LEMURIA
A CIVILIZATION TIME FORGOT

UNA MARCOTTE

BALBOA.
PRESS
A DIVISION OF HAY HOUSE

Balboa Press books may be ordered through booksellers or by contacting:

Balboa Press
A Division of Hay House
1663 Liberty Drive
Bloomington, IN 47403
www.balboapress.com
1 (877) 407-4847

Print information available on the last page.

ISBN: 978-1-9822-0641-3 (sc)
ISBN: 978-1-9822-0642-0 (e)

Balboa Press rev. date: 10/24/2018

CONTENTS

INTRODUCTION

I walked into the lobby of the A.R.E.'s Visitor Center one morning and immediately paused to look into the bookstore in search of new books on display. Today, one caught my eye. This book just jumped out at me crying "buy me, buy me." Since I couldn't read the title, I had to contain my curiosity until the bookstore opened. As it turned out, the book was *The Lost Continent of Mu* by James Churchward. I knew very little of Mu or Lemuria as it is most popularly called today, so I decided to buy it. Although I must confess that it was the most boring book I've ever read, it nevertheless changed the course of my life because for the next 20 years, I became almost obsessed to find reliable sources on the topic of Lemuria.

My search began at the world's second largest metaphysical library, the A.R.E. Library in Virginia Beach, with an examination of the Edgar Cayce readings. The first pass was disappointing because only 16 readings contained any relevant information. I learned that the Edgar Cayce readings linked Lemuria and Mu as one and the same place; that it was a matriarchal society; and that Lemurians had settled the American southwest as Churchward had already stated. It was not a lot of information, so both the Cayce readings and the Churchward book sat together on one side of my desk for several years.

Meanwhile, I continued my search in the Egerton Sykes book and magazine collection the A.R.E library acquired several years earlier. Sykes was a British journalist and writer who collected everything that had ever been written on the subject of Atlantis and Lemuria. Browsing through the collection took over a year and I did find that the Rudolf Steiner books on Atlantis and Lemuria, although very difficult to comprehend, contained some helpful information.

Finally, I accidentally stumbled across Wishar Cerve's book entitled *Lemuria* in the library's reserve section. When I learned from Cerve's book that the Baja Peninsula along with California were once a part of Lemuria, I thought "Wow! I doubt many people in this world know that California was not originally a part of North America!" Moreover, I found corroboration of that information in the Cayce readings even though the word "Lemuria" did not appear in the reading at all. And this "find" encouraged me to continue my research. With the addition of Cerve's book, I had enough material to provide a sketch of Lemuria and its history although I felt uneasy because the information I gathered lacked some depth. Nevertheless, the first draft of a book on the subject of this prehistoric civilization was born and subsequently bought by the ARE Press.

While the book languished on a shelf in the ARE Press division for several years, more resources came to my attention. First, Shirley MacLaine published her book entitled *The Camino* in 2000. Although her main focus was her spiritual journey walking across the Camino road in northern Spain, I was surprised at how much information she accessed during meditation about life in Lemuria. Her description of the events that occurred during Lemuria's final destruction were riveting. Another year went by and an audience member in one of my lectures on Lemuria asked if I were familiar with a book entitled *The Lemurian Way* by Lauren Thyme and Sareya Orion. I was very pleased at having been made aware of this source for the material the authors presented included detailed information on Lemurian lifestyle and way of thinking, both of which differ drastically from modern times. Armed with a better understanding of the Lemurian culture, I was ready to retrieve my first manuscript and revise it.

Finally, the last source fell into place as I started draft #2. Journalist Ruth Montgomery's book, *The World to Come*, filled a big hole as far as presenting a complete picture of the Lemurian saga. That missing piece of research was migration and this source answered the question of where the Lemurians went when they knew their continent would be imminently destroyed. The story was now complete.

For those readers interested only in the story of Lemuria, I invite them to read the first section of Chapter 1 and move right into Chapter

3. On the other hand, those readers who want to know how all of us came to planet earth, how souls became trapped down here, then Chapter 2 on the journey of the soul would be of interest.

The Lemurians are known in the ancient world for developing the brain. Moreover, there are several conflicting opinions on Lemurians and the brain – such as, did the Lemurians even have one? Chapter 6 deals with this topic, including the controversy as to whether or not members of the Lemurian civilization did or did not possess a brain.

The Lemurian civilization existed so long ago why would it be relevant to learn about it today? It is relevant because the Lemurians had been a highly spiritual society, exhibiting cooperation, compassion, joyfulness, and unconditional love to each other. This is the consciousness level the modern world is slowly returning to. This is the Ascension everyone has been speculating about and waiting for. It is a change in thinking. It's an elevation of the mind and emotions, not the body. It is the Lemurian energy at its highest vibration returning to planet earth for the first time since the continent disappeared under the Pacific Ocean over 52,000 years ago.

If there is any doubt major change is upon us, I invite people to look around at the results of the shift from the patriarchal to matriarchal energy in the time Donald Trump took office in early 2017. In a little over a year, more women have run for political office than at any previous time in history; sexual harassment charges are taken seriously and many prominent men have lost their jobs in the twinkling of eye; and equal pay for women is making progress in the media industry where it will trickle into other jobs and positions. That is major progress towards a higher consciousness.

Therefore, may the return of the vibrant and joyous Lemurian energy continue to increase and prevail on planet earth and may we all enjoy and reap the rewards of its return.

Una Marcotte
Virginia Beach, Virginia
2018

MYTH, LEGEND, OR HISTORY?

Once upon a time, a solid land mass covered most of the Pacific Ocean. Some call the vanished continent Lemuria. Some call it Mu. Whatever name you would like to use, Lemuria or Mu existed before recorded history and its beginnings occurred prior to the more famously known ancient civilization of Atlantis. Not a trace of Lemuria or Mu can be found today, but whispers of its possibility remains through legends and myths as well as references in paranormal sources. Some believe that all that has survived of this sunken continent are its lofty mountain tops known today as the Polynesian Islands. Although plausible, this theory cannot be proved scientifically. It can only be believed or at least considered a probability.

It is not the intent of this book to prove the existence of Lemuria. Rather it is meant to be a compilation of many sources that together may point to the possibility that a land mass once existed in the Pacific Ocean many thousands of years ago. It provided a home to what would be considered today an unusual civilization and, although very different from modern times, a very advanced society even by today's standards.

Although most people call it Lemuria, the continent probably had another name that is now forgotten. The word "Lemuria" came to be associated with this part of the world when scientists in the mid-1800's found a species of monkeys known as *lemurs*, which resembled a cross between a monkey and a squirrel. Lemurs have a human-looking face, and it was once believed that they were part of the evolutionary line for the human race. They are not. However, the lemurs are still prevalent on the island of Madagascar off the coast of Africa as well as on the African mainland, in India and Indonesia. Scientists speculated that, in order to have the lemurs inhabiting all these varied, unconnected areas, there once must have been a land bridge for them to traverse. In 1870, an English zoologist, Philip L. Sclater, gave the submerged lands of the Indian Ocean the name "Lemuria" in honor of the lemurs. Although no one ever formally declared "Lemuria" as the official name for this submerged area, continual usage over time made the name synonymous with this lost landmass and the civilization who resided there.

In the 1930's, a retired British colonel, James Churchward, gave the name Mu to the lost land mass in the Pacific. An inventor and engineer, Churchward spent the latter part of his life trying to prove Mu's existence. He claimed to have found the name "Mu" on ancient tablets hidden in a monastery where he resided for a short time while he was stationed in India. No one else has ever seen these tablets, so his word that these ancient lands were known as Mu is all that is available. (More about Churchward later.)

Although the zoologist Sclater probably meant to use the term Lemuria for just the sunken land in the Indian Ocean, the name came to be associated with the lost continent of the Pacific Ocean as well. Some people even make a distinction between Lemuria and Mu, and consider the lands under the Indian Ocean as Lemuria and the lands under the Pacific Ocean as Mu. All that is certain is that both the areas in the Pacific Ocean and those in the Indian Ocean were once one large, connected land mass. That would make Lemuria a predecessor of not only the Polynesian Islands but also Japan, Australia, New Zealand, the Indonesian Islands, India, Tibet, Ceylon, and Madagascar. For the purposes of this book, popular usage will be honored, and the name Lemuria will refer to the lost lands in both the Pacific and Indian Oceans.

One might ask if there is no scientific proof that Lemuria ever really existed, then where can information concerning this civilization be found. References to Lemuria and its people for the most part reside in material from channeled and other paranormal sources. Since not all of these types of sources are completely reliable, each source should be evaluated as to whether or not the information has some authentication. One way to verify paranormal information is to cross check the data with either historical or other reliable paranormal sources. When more than one of these sources agree on a certain point, the information receives a higher rate of validity and presents a greater possibility of being true. The following sections in this chapter will examine several of the more prominent paranormal sources who have contributed the larger body of information regarding the ancient civilization of Lemuria.

Madame Blavatsky (1831-1891)

While members of the scientific community gave the lost continent its name, the occult community brought it to public attention. In 1888, Madame Helena Petrovna Blavatsky, founder of the Theosophical Society, published her third book, *The Secret Doctrine*, where she imparted the ancient wisdom shared with her by the Brotherhood of the Mahatmas — ethereal beings who made their home in Tibet. According to them, the Lemurians occupied the land stretching from the Himalayas to the Antarctic Circle, a rather large portion of the then known world.

Madame Blavatsky called the lost continent of the Pacific and Indian Oceans Lemuria (not Mu) and reported that the Lemurians belonged to the "third root race." A root race is a term that designates the large periods of time marking the various stages in human evolution. According to the Theosophists, there will be seven root races, each composed of seven sub races. Modern man belongs to the fifth root race, and Blavatsky claimed that the sixth root race will evolve from the present *Homo sapiens*, returning to live in Lemuria.

The Lemurians are described in Blavatsky's book as gigantic, apelike creatures with no brains. She claimed that some Lemurians had four arms and some had an eye on the back of their head. It was this "eye" that gave them their psychic vision. Lemurians communicated telepathically and used no language at all. While some of them made their homes in caves, others dug huge holes in the ground to use as homes. Although they were brainless, Blavatsky claimed that the Lemurians could use their willpower to move large objects, including mountains. Although it does not seem to fit the current scientific timeframe, she reports that the Lemurian continent was destroyed 40 million years ago, and that the Australian Aborigines are among their descendants.

Ironically, Blavatsky retracted all of the information she received from the Brotherhood before she died, so her material on Lemuria and Lemurians is all the more questionable. Today, she is not considered a credible source on any subject and for this reason, Blavatsky's material is not a main source of information for this book. However, she is mentioned here because she deserves to be recognized as one of the first persons to treat the topic of Lemuria seriously and the first to leave extensive personal writings about the lost civilization even though her information is now in doubt because of her retraction.

William Scott-Elliot (18? - 1930)

This British Theosophist added to Madame Blavatsky's information on Lemuria by receiving revelations from the "Theosophical Masters," whose information he incorporated into his book entitled *The Story of Atlantis and Lost Lemuria*. He claimed to have received copies of world maps of that ancient era, which also appear in the book. The real sources for the maps were never revealed, and they have not received much attention.

As for the Lemurians, Scott-Elliot described them as 12 to 15 feet tall with a flat face, no forehead, but a protruding muzzle. They were brown-skinned with eyes set so wide apart that they could see both sideways and forward. He confirmed Blavatsky's claim to the third eye in the back of the head, and added that this eye was most useful to the Lemurians as they had elongated heels and could walk backward as easily as forward.

Scott-Elliot claimed that the Lemurians were androgynous and reproduced by laying eggs. Actually, he used the term "hermaphrodite" rather than "androgynous." He claimed that eventually the Lemurians evolved to reproducing the way mammals did. During their sexual development, says Scott-Elliot, the Lemurians interfered with the animal kingdom by interbreeding with them. This interference interrupted a more highly evolved plan to advance toward some form of human body type. Eventually, Scott-Elliot claimed that beings from Venus influenced the Lemurian race to develop into an advanced civilization and to breed into a more recognizable human form.

Much of Scott-Elliot's information sounds very far-fetched, and it did not make the Lemurians sound very appealing. This unattractive look at Lemuria is probably one of the reasons why many people did not pursue any in-depth examination of this slice of human history. Some of Scott-Elliot's theories do show up in other paranormal sources on Lemuria, but his works are best brought forth as supporting information. Since there is much skepticism surrounding all of the theories Scott-Elliot put forth, probably because of his affiliation with Madame Blavatsky, his works will not serve as a main source of information for this book but rather as a corroborative source.

Rudolf Steiner (1861-1925)

Austrian philosopher and educator Rudolf Steiner was a Theosophist until 1907 when he left the organization to form his own Anthroposophical Society. He published his book *Cosmic Memory: Atlantis and Lemuria* in 1923, claiming his information came from the Akashic Records, a term that defines the chronicles or records of each and every soul's activities and progress since creation. Steiner maintained that these records can be accessed only by an "initiate" — someone who has received special training to tap into the spiritual world.

Many feel that Steiner's information on Lemuria was influenced by Madame Blavatsky. He agreed with other Theosophists in that the Lemurians were androgynous until the earth became more compact. This increased density forced the division of the sexes, splitting the androgynous body into a male and female form, a change he claims the Lemurians did not willingly support. In fact, Steiner reported that especially after the separation into male and female bodies, they considered sexual contact a sacred duty rather than a pleasure. Moreover, as humans began to settle themselves into their new body types, Steiner explains that the Lemurians taught their men to bear pain as a way to develop will power. The women were placed outdoors during storms to "feel" the many vibrations that are increased through storms to help the females refine their intuitive skills.

According to Steiner, the Lemurians used their will power to lift heavy objects. They also evolved the body's vision and speech abilities to a higher degree from its original capabilities. Although their brains could not reason yet, they had tremendous memory capacity. To his credit, Steiner left much information on the evolution of the brain which became highly developed during the Lemurian times. His information on Lemuria, and Atlantis as well, gives valuable insights into both of these ancient civilizations. His material on the brain will be examined in more detail in chapter 6.

Edgar Cayce (1877-1945)

Considered a psychic, Edgar Cayce, who died in 1945, left behind an incredible legacy of documented information on over 10,000 topics including ancient civilizations. The accuracy of his information, especially in the health field, has stood the test of time and proved to be consistently truthful and highly accurate.

Born in Hopkinsville, Kentucky in 1877, Edgar Cayce as a young man discovered that he could go into an altered state of consciousness and answer specific questions posed to him. He is not considered a channeler as no other entity entered his body during his trance state. In fact, he used his own voice to transmit information while other channelers report that they step aside to have an entity use their body including their vocal chords. Instead, Cayce used self-hypnosis and appeared to be asleep while he imparted the requested information. In fact, he came to be known to the world as the "sleeping prophet" after Jess Stern, the famous author and journalist, entitled his biography of Cayce *The Sleeping Prophet*. It was published in the early 1960's and became a New York Times best-seller.

Cayce had the foresight to document his sessions. He had a stenographer in the room each time he answered questions posed to him by people who were either present for their reading or sent their questions to him through the mail. These questions and answers became known as "readings" and are now catalogued, numbered, computerized, and made available to the public through the organization founded by Cayce in 1931 known as the Association for Research and Enlightenment (A.R.E.), located in Virginia Beach, Virginia.

Cayce did not remember anything that transpired during his self-imposed trance state and had to wait for his stenographer, Gladys Davis, to transcribe her notes to find out what questions were asked and answered. Davis always made two copies of her transcriptions — one was sent to the person requesting the reading, while the second copy was kept by the Cayce family and eventually by the Edgar Cayce Foundation. These original copies are still retained in their archives, copies available to the public at the A.R.E. library.

When Cayce discovered his abilities in the early 1920's, he thought his gift only centered on giving physical health readings for people. Although he had no medical training, in his altered state he apparently could read a person's body as though he had x-ray eyes, and he proposed treatments for any inappropriate condition encountered. Later, it was accidentally discovered that he could answer questions asked that were unrelated to physical health. It was this realization that eventually led to what are presently known as "life readings."

The life readings gave people information on the past lives that affected their present one. This material brought the possibility of reincarnation to the forefront, a concept that Cayce and his family struggled with before accepting its possibility. In fact, the reliability of his information on past lives made many who have studied the readings believers in the reincarnation process.

To obtain requested information for a life reading, Cayce claimed to reach the soul's record. He called that source the Akashic Records. Cayce's information from those records — the same records Steiner claimed to be able to read — provided people with their successes and set-backs in previous lives along with the attitudes and patterns developed during those lifetimes that needed to be changed in the present. Life readings contained references to ancient civilizations no one knew anything about, including the civilizations of Da, Og, Oz, La, Ur, Atlantis, and of course, Lemuria or Mu.

A search of the computerized Cayce readings using the words "Lemuria" and "Mu" results in over 90 responses to the query. Unfortunately, all but 16 of these readings simply mention that a person was alive or knew someone from Lemuria or Mu in a past life. Even the 16 readings that contain more information do not offer much detail about life in Lemuria or Mu. For that reason, the Cayce readings are often passed over as an important source of information on this ancient civilization.

What many researchers do not realize is that information on ancient civilizations is often buried in the Cayce readings. For example, the startling information that the Baja Peninsula and parts of California were once a part of the continent of Lemuria does not appear on the results of a keyword search of "Lemuria" or "Mu" because these words are not in that reading. For this reason, it takes time and a great deal of ingenuity and effort to really research the Cayce readings. Nevertheless, because of their high rate of accuracy, the time spent in researching here can be well worth the effort and can also be helpful when evaluating the validity of channeled material from others. For these reasons, the Cayce readings provide a pivotal source in this book for dealing with information on Lemuria.

To make individual people's readings available to the public, the Edgar Cayce Foundation replaced names with numbers to maintain anonymity for those seeking a reading. Therefore, whenever a reading number is included in this book, the first numbers simply replace the name of the person obtaining the reading. The numbers that follow the hyphen indicate the number of the reading this person received, as some people obtained more than one reading. For example, while the 294 in Cayce reading 294-2 represents a person's name, the 2 following the dash denotes that this is the person's second reading from Cayce.

James M. Churchward (1851-1936)

Rejected by the scientific community in his lifetime, the ideas of the previously mentioned James Churchward are making a comeback in popularity today. Several journalists who reported on the underwater discoveries of ancient structures near Japan in 1995 included Churchward's name as a major source of information regarding these ancient sites now buried under the sea. A few even went so far as to link Mu to the underwater city that covers nearly 311 miles near Okinawa and beyond the island of Yonaguni. Although the discovery put Lemuria in the forefront again, a study of Lemurian life-style shows that this civilization didn't erect large structures. Therefore, these recently discovered sizable man-made platforms and stone archways found underwater near Japan along with those found near Cuba and the island of Bimini are all probably remnants of Atlantean construction.

Churchward wrote five books on Lemuria or Mu and had extensive notes for a sixth one that was eventually published in 1997, long after his death. These book titles include *The Lost Continent of Mu*, *Motherland of Man*, *The Children of Mu*, *The Sacred Symbols of Mu*, and *Cosmic Forces of Mu*. Churchward used the name Mu exclusively in his writings and advocated that the lost continent of Mu now forms the ocean floor for the Pacific Ocean. He offered proof of Mu's existence in various ways, but mostly through symbols found on pottery, recovered walls and pillars of temple decorations found in Mexico, buried tablets also found in Mexico, and stone markers or rock formations in the American Southwest. His proof even included linking the symbols used in the ancient alphabets of such countries as Greece and India with the symbols associated with Mu.

Although his information intrigued the general public and armchair anthropologists, by the time Churchward published his books on Mu, he had antagonized too many important people in the influential social strata. This rift may be a key contributing factor to the ridicule his work on Mu met on the scientific front. The major cause of this antagonism was the lawsuit victories Churchward and his long-time friend and patent attorney, Percy Tate Griffith, won against Carnegie Steel in 1910 and Bethlehem Steel in 1915. Churchward, an engineer, had invented a fine steel known in the industry as NCV Steel that was lightweight yet strong enough to be used in the construction of warships. Other steel companies had infringed on his patent and were already selling it to the American government. Churchward was blackballed out of the steel industry after his court victories, forcing him and Griffith to sell the invention to a small steel company. However, the court victories gave Churchward the money he needed to pursue his first love, namely finding proof of the existence of Mu.

Another contributing factor to the mistrust of Churchward's information on Mu by the experts was their inability to prove the source of his claims of where he learned the symbols of Mu. According to Churchward, he studied these symbols from ancient Naacal (displaced people from the lost continent of Lemuria) tablets and was taught their translations by his hosts during his stay in a monastery while stationed in India with the British army. Yet, when others returned to this same monastery to authenticate the existence of these tablets, the monks would not admit them and denied any existence of these tablets. With this turn of events, Churchward's credibility was lost until modern times.

It was adventurer David Hatcher Childress, author of *Lost Cities of Ancient Lemuria and the Pacific*, who pointed out that the Rosicrucian Order of San Jose, California, claims to have access to a number of secret libraries hidden all over Tibet. If that is the case, says Childress, then Churchward's secret Mu tablets are not so unbelievable, especially in light of the additional discovery that monks in India are highly selective about which people are actually admitted to their monasteries. In other words, while Churchward had gained the monks' trust, those researchers that followed asking to see the same tablets were denied access because the monks decided they would not be admitted for one reason or another.

Although there is information in the Churchward books that cannot be authenticated or verified, new discoveries and technology have solidified some of his theories and advanced his credibility. In almost any mention of Lemuria today, Churchward is referenced and oftentimes considered an important source on the lost continent of the Pacific even though he is still not fully sanctioned by the scientific community.

Wishar S. Cerve (Harvey Spencer Lewis, 1883-1939)

The Rosicrucian Order, also known as the Ancient and Mystical Order of the Rose Cross (AMORC), is dedicated to preserving ancient teachings of the natural and metaphysical sciences to develop the higher faculties of the human being. In 1931, the organization published a book entitled *Lemuria* written under the name Wishar Cerve. As it turns out, Wishar Cerve was a pseudonym for Harvey Spencer Lewis, the founder of the Rosicrucian Order in California.

The introduction of this book elaborately told the tale that the Rosicrucians approached Cerve, supposedly a Frenchman by birth, to write a book on the fascinating facts concerning Lemuria found in the rare manuscripts preserved in the secret archives of Tibet and China. His mission was to present non-technical aspects of the ancient civilization, concentrating on the human elements of the Lemurian lifestyle. (Incidentally, author Lewis was actually born in *French*town, New Jersey.)

Cerve lived up to his "assignment" by creating an idealistic view of Lemurians. As far as appearance, he perpetuated the Lemurian body-types depicted by the Theosophists, adding almost romantic reasons surrounding their odd features of an eye in the back of the head and extra-long heels. Moreover, he went beyond the ancient manuscripts by proliferating the mythical stories surrounding the Lemurians making Mt. Shasta in California their present-day home, hiding themselves inside the mountain and thus rarely seen by modern man.

Nevertheless, Cerve's book is worth its place among the collection of Lemurian sources as it offered several intriguing concepts among the myths and legends. One of the unique pieces of information included a series of maps showing the shapes of the land masses above water during Lemurian times. These maps differ from any other ancient maps presented by the Theosophists, but are in sync with information found in the Cayce readings and the maps proposed by James Churchward. The second distinctive concept suggested in this book is that the state of California was once a part of the continent of Lemuria. As far-fetched as that seems, Cerve presented respectable arguments in support of his theory. Moreover, his hypothesis is also supported by information found in the Cayce readings and thus has a strong possibility of being correct.

Additional Sources

There continues to be a variety of sources contributing information about Lemuria. On the academic front, the science of DNA may eventually replace archeological digs to prove the existence of past civilizations. For instance, Greg and Laura Little in their book *Ancient South America* point to research that provides evidence through the study of DNA that the people of the Pacific originated from a group of islands in the southwestern portion of the Pacific known as Melanesia and nearby Indonesia. Moreover, the Littles wrote that because the people of the South Pacific inhabited these islands for so long, it is estimated by the experts that their place of origin is their present location. Although no one has come forth to admit that this research based on DNA may someday be a part of the proof that a Lemurian civilization once existed there, these possibilities are now at least under discussion.

On the paranormal side, people every day are stepping forward to share information they've received through channeling, visions, past-life regressions, meditation, and even dreams. Some of these sources are well-known, such as the channeler, Lazaris; Seth channeled by Jane Roberts; Abraham channeled by Esther Hicks; the Lemurian Elders channeled by Lauren Thyme; and automatic writer, Ruth Montgomery, to name a few. Even film star Shirley MacLaine has shared many of her past life insights received through channelers such as Kevin Ryerson and from her own deep meditative experiences. In fact, in her book *The Camino*, MacLaine included a valuable piece of information when she described experiencing her androgynous body splitting into its male and female parts, an event which will be examined in more detail in Chapter 2 of this book.

Other sources of information come from ordinary men and women catching glimpses of their own past experiences through one paranormal method or another. Anthropologist Kathy Callahan,

Ph.D., in her book *Our Origin and Destiny* points out that more humans are developing a sixth sense today that goes beyond the five accepted physical senses. She sees the development of this extra sense as a sign of an evolutionary human change, one of greater psychic and intuitive abilities that will soon be manifested by everyone. Therefore, it should come as no surprise that more and more information on Lemuria will appear in the coming years as people's intuitive capabilities increase. New information from such sources is always welcomed, especially if it adds yet another piece to the overall puzzle surrounding Lemuria.

Truthfully, proving that Lemuria existed beyond a shadow of a doubt may never happen. The main land area of Lemuria has been under water for so long that providing physical proof through accepted scientific data would be enormously difficult as water, especially salt water, can erode traces of civilization rather quickly. Turning to paranormal sources for proof often seems the only alternative to find information about any prerecorded civilization, even though many people often dismiss these sources as being too imaginative.

There is an emerging and encouraging trend, however, towards a greater acceptance of information provided through paranormal means, perhaps because as Dr. Callahan pointed out, many more people are developing their intuitive skills themselves. The greater acceptance of paranormal sources will allow researchers to present more cohesive theories on the Lemurian way of life by finding the common threads among the various sources. Although these concepts may not be scientifically verifiable, the same information repeated from more than one paranormal source can point lovers of ancient mysteries towards some semblance of possible universal truth of life and events on earth before recorded history.

It is hoped that this particular "common thread" compiled through the myriad information from several reliable paranormal sources described in this chapter will present at least one credible view of the Lemurians, their lifestyle, their beliefs, and their demise. Their unfolding story in the following pages should present a fascinating read and perhaps even considered a possible trustworthy snapshot in time of this mysterious and little known ancient civilization from Lemuria.

THE SOUL'S JOURNEY TO LEMURIA

One of the first questions on everyone's mind when they first hear about Lemuria is when did it exist? No one knows for sure. As of this writing, no channeler, no psychic, not even archeologists can offer any accurate timeline for the Lemurian civilization. As mentioned in the previous chapter, occultists Blavatsky and Scott-Elliott claimed the Lemurians existed 40 million years ago. Their timeframe is soundly rejected by the scientific community as the present anthropological discoveries verify that humans appeared much later. So far, fossil specimens linked to the human evolutionary line date back to 4.1 million years ago. Maeve G. Leakey and her research team uncovered this oldest specimen in 1994 at Lake Turkana in northern Kenya.

If the importance of an accurate timeline for the existence of Lemuria can be set aside for a moment, probable dates for this civilization might be estimated through the use of the Edgar Cayce readings. Although not always on the mark when dealing with future time, this source has proved more accurate than most when dealing with events of the past. An example of this assessment lies with the 10, 500 B.C. timeframe the Cayce readings provided as the building date for the Great Pyramid of Egypt on the Giza plateau. Obviously, this date does not match the official ones of 3,000 to 4,000 B.C. the Egyptologists support. That the Edgar Cayce readings erred was the common assumption until John Anthony West and Robert Bauval entered the picture.

West, an author and life-long student of Egypt's ancient heritage, offered proof that the Sphinx on the Giza Plateau existed more than 12,000 years ago in a 1993 NBC documentary entitled *The Mystery of the Sphinx*. He pointed out that the pattern of the erosion marks on the monument were formed by water, probably during heavy and long periods of rainfall. He found that such a weather phenomenon occurred over 12,000 years ago. West's contribution to the dating efforts of the Giza plateau is substantiated in the Cayce readings where it was recorded that the Sphinx already existed on the Giza Plateau when the building of the Great Pyramid began in 10,600 B.C. The readings claimed that the Great Pyramid was completed in 10,500 B.C., taking 100 years to build.

In 1994, Bauval, a Belgium-born engineer, offered the hypothesis that the lay-out of the three pyramids at Giza mirrored the stars forming the belt in the constellation of Orion. The belt contains two stars side-by-side with the belt's third star slightly off the alignment. The misaligned pyramid on the Giza plateau puzzled the experts for years. Since the ancient ones built with such perfect engineering and mathematical precision, they must also have possessed the knowledge and skill to align all three pyramids perfectly. So why didn't they build in one straight line? Bauval's theory explained the probable reason for the third pyramid's misalignment through the use of the computerized Skyglobe astrological program as a tool. Bauval illustrated that Orion's belt hovered directly above the Giza plateau around 10,500 B.C., a date that matches the one given in the readings rather than the one supported by Egyptian archeologists. Therefore, one can safely conclude that the pyramid builders possibly built the pyramids on the Giza Plateau to match the stars above, or "as above, so below," during the 10,500 B.C. timeframe, proving the Cayce readings also were right on target.

Although anthropologists still have not sanctioned these dates, the example helps support the possibility that dates found in the Edgar Cayce readings are quite reliable. With that in mind, let's start by using logic to establish an approximate beginning point for the Lemurian age. Firstly, according to the Cayce readings, Atlantis existed for 200,000 thousand years. Therefore, if the final Atlantean destruction, again according to the Cayce readings, occurred near the time the Great Pyramid was built or somewhere between 10,500 B.C. and 9,500 B.C., the date offered by the Greek philosopher, Plato, then the beginning date for the Atlantean civilization can be calculated at approximately 210,500 B.C.

Secondly, both the Cayce readings and the Akashic Record readings of Rudolf Steiner indicated that the Lemurian civilization was older than the one in Atlantis. In fact, some experts of these ancient civilizations believe that Atlantis was a colony of Lemuria, but neither of these sources verified such a relationship. Nor did they offer any information on how long the Lemurian civilization lasted. The only clue these sources left behind to help with a start date is that Lemuria existed before Atlantis. Based on that information and knowing an approximate start date for Atlantis, the appearance of the Lemurian civilization may be as early as 300,000 to 250,000 B.C. Although there is no precise start date for Lemuria, there is an end date. Ruth Montgomery and her guides wrote in her book, *The World Before*, that the destruction of Lemuria happened in 48,000 B.C.

Based on the deductions presented, approximate dates are now available to answer the question of when Lemuria did exist. The answer is probably between 300,000 to 48,000 B.C. These dates fall within the range of the Paleolithic era, more precisely the Middle Paleolithic age whose years span the dates from 300,000 to 30,000 BC.

Lemuria in the Paleolithic Age

The scientific community documented that during this timeframe, Neanderthal sapiens became prevalent in Europe and the Homo sapiens, a more modern human body-type, emerged throughout the known world. At this time, people began to group together to form small societies. They started to engage in religious and spiritual behavior such as burial rites and other rituals. Artistic expression also emerged during this era in the form of cave drawings, rock art, and jewelry. Fire was already invented. Those societies existing in colder climates hunted wild animals for food and had already learned how to cook meat. Other societies in milder climates survived by gathering plants and fishing.

This archeological description of the Paleolithic human lifestyle complements paranormal information for the start of the Lemurian civilization. Although the scientific world provides a good picture of how people lived during this age, there is more to consider than just the physical existence. What archeologists do not take into consideration that paranormal sources do is the role the spiritual soul played at this time. There are two parallel energies at work to enhance the view of the historical past – one with the evolutionary aspects of the physical forms and the other with the spiritual side of those forms during this evolutionary process.

Although it is generally believed and taught by western religions that Adam and Eve were the first humans, the Bible does hint that others also inhabited the earth at the same time. In Genesis, the couple received the caution of not to mix the sons of God [themselves and their descendants] with the daughters of men [other body types]. In other words, they were asked to keep their new body structure (or bloodline) pure. That there were other souls in different body structures on earth before Adam and Eve arrived on the scene implies that the Bible did not include the complete story of the soul's development on earth. Therefore, it is also possible that the history of the soul's journey on earth did not begin with Adam and Eve either.

If the Bible is not a main source to study the soul's evolvement into matter, then where does one start looking for the history of the soul's spiritual heritage? Probably the Akashic Records which serve as the storage area for each individual soul record since creation. The challenge is to find a source who can read the ethereal Akashic Records accurately. Fortunately, two such reliable resources do exist, namely the Edgar Cayce readings and Steiner's Akashic readings on Atlantis and Lemuria. Diverting briefly into the Akashic Records to obtain a better understanding of the beginnings or creation will explain the larger spiritual picture that influenced the Lemurian civilization, a viewpoint that the scientific community does not take into consideration.

Creation of the Soul

Before looking into the topic of creation, consider for a moment that Western thought centers around the perception that we are human beings with a soul, placing the emphasis on the human or physical first. This perspective came with the Greek philosophers who greatly admired the mind with its logical thinking processes. They ushered in the age of reason and supported logical thinking over the intuitive process, erasing the knowledge that intuition is the birthright of human beings as it is a part of the soul. As the logical or scientific method of thinking could not really prove the existence of the soul, then the philosophical question arises of whether or not a soul really exists. The mind has played with this puzzling question for a couple thousand years now without any satisfactory or definitive conclusions.

Enter the Cayce readings to say "yes," there really is a soul and offer details on its activities since the time of creation. According to the Cayce readings taken from the Akashic Records, God created souls for a rather simple reason: the Creator desired companionship and moved (Edgar Cayce reading 263-13). In that moment of movement, the Creator generated all souls and fashioned them in His/Her image as stated in the Bible. This means that the image of God's light or energy patterns mirrored themselves in the newly created souls and since God or the Creator, as He/She will be called in this book, did not have a physical body, neither did the souls. Therefore, the created souls most probably took an androgynous form, containing both male and female aspects of the Creator who is genderless, an androgynous Spirit Himself/Herself.

The souls also received from the Creator an individual consciousness with a great capacity to love, an ability to manifest anything focused upon, and gifted with a free will. In fact, it is the gift of free will that sets souls apart from plant and animal life, making souls a unique form in the creation hierarchy. Moreover, the Creator did not generate souls to blindly follow their Maker. With their free will, souls constantly do initiate their choice as to whether or not to follow their Creator's directives, not because they have to but because of their love for the One who produced them out of a desire for their companionship.

The Edgar Cayce readings claimed that all souls were created at the same time and studying the readings regarding creation one arrives to the conclusion that creating body and soul together did not happen. The soul was created first and THEN entered a body much later in time. To say it another way, human beings are primarily souls undergoing a human experience, not the other way around as many people are taught to believe.

Dr. Shakuntala Modi, a board certified psychologist using hypnosis to help her patients, expressed surprise at learning that people could be regressed to the time of creation. In her findings, published in *Memories of God and Creation* in 2000, Dr. Modi reports that her patients described the Creator before creation as a big ball of golden light surrounded by darkness. Within that ball of light, they saw a creative energy force in constant motion. While most people reported seeing the Creator as a ball of light, a few saw a pyramid while still others claimed He/She appeared divided into sections much like the spokes in a wheel. Whatever the description of the Creator's form, all were unanimous that the Creator appeared as light in a black void.

When Dr. Modi asked her patients why God decided to create souls, the majority answered that it was because the Creator felt lonely. Others replied that He/She wanted to experience love through creation and thus created souls to communicate with and to help them grow through love. Still another group of people saw that as the Creator grew and expanded, parts of Himself/Herself, hereafter called souls, left the protection of Creator's light, and reattached themselves through cords as the Creator did not want the wandering souls to remain lonely in the void. No matter how the reasons are worded, companionship seems to be at the core of the prime motivation for the decision to generate souls.

Both the Cayce readings and Dr. Modi's regressed patients report that the Creator produced multiple universes for the new souls to explore. Secure in the Creator's love and affection, some souls remained close while others investigated the far reaches of these universes, returning to the safety of the Creator through protective pathways that Dr. Modi's patients referred to as tunnels, channels, or rays. What both sources make clear is that no location was ever meant to be a permanent residence for the souls. However, through the use of their free will, certain souls took the option to continually visit certain areas available to them.

One of the locales that became a magnet for certain souls was the planet earth. They became fascinated with the plant and animal life here, and this attraction changed the Creator's ultimate plan. While the souls' intent was just to experience the earth, eventually they began to meddle with the natural evolution in progress here.

Unfortunately, many souls became so infatuated with this planet that not only did they return again and again but remained for longer and longer periods of time. Groups of souls began to work together to evolve certain species of animal and plant life, even creating new varieties. They probably accomplished all this through the manipulation of the DNA of animals and plant life although still respecting their Creator enough to work within the patterns for the species already set. Thousands or perhaps even millions of earth years passed in this way with souls remaining indefinitely on the planet earth in their spirit form engrossed in their evolutionary projects of the flora and fauna.

Root Races

The occultists and Rudolf Steiner's channeling efforts presented the evolution of the current human body form through root races, a term not generally used in people's vocabulary today. A root race is simply a variation or change in the human body type or structure. The Edgar Cayce readings defined the Root Races not just from a physical standpoint but also from a spiritual viewpoint. In comparison, the Theosophists offer detail information on the evolution of only the human body itself. The Edgar Cayce perspective of the Root Races are simpler to understand as they were divided according to the methods souls used to enter into matter. For the purposes of this book, the souls' evolvement into matter will center on the readings' perspective of the Root Races and not the rather detailed and complex divisions the Theosophists offer.

According to the students of the Edgar Cayce readings, there are four root races. The First Root Race was called "spirit", indicating that souls coming into the earth plane did not have physical bodies at first. They remained in their original state of creation, in the image of the Creator or spirit's androgynous form.

The Second Root Race indicated the period of time souls created bodies to use to experience the earth or for the simple pleasure of experimenting and utilizing their own creative process. This Second Root Race was called "thought form" in the Cayce readings, as souls would "think" up bodies to create. The Third Root Race occurred when the souls discovered "projection", the ability to project themselves in and out of existing physical bodies at will. Finally, the Fourth Root Race, which also became known as the Adamic root race, began when the Creator requested that souls occupy bodies that were specifically created for their use while on earth. The Fourth Root Race began the history of the Homo sapiens' journey in the earth, and according to the Bible, began with the creation of Adam and eventually Eve.

The appearance of one root race did not necessarily negate the existence of the previous one. It is possible that the Second, Third, and Fourth Root Races were in existence all at the same time. Eventually, usage of the Second and Third Root Races disappeared, leaving only the Fourth Root Race's new body-type in existence. The Fourth Root Race's body-type, with some modifications evolving over time, is the same body-type human beings use today, just denser than in Lemurian times. However, the Edgar Cayce readings do warn that humanity will imminently evolve into a Fifth Root Race, and although no specific timeframe is available for this experience, the readings indicate that the transition to a new body-type will happen not that far into the future.

Creation of Thought Forms – the Second Root Race

Returning to the creation timeline, souls began to realize over time that they could not thoroughly enjoy what the earth had to offer while still in their spirit form. They realized that they did not have the sense of touch to feel the texture of a leaf, the rough bark of a tree, or the soft fur of an animal. As they observed animals eating, they realized they did not know how any edible plant or the fruits of a plant tasted. Without olfactory capabilities, they could not even smell the perfume of the blooming flowers around them. Feeling deprived of the ability to totally experience earth in these ways, souls realized they needed some kind of physical form.

Their first solution was to think up bodies to use since the souls had the power to create anything they focused on, one of their gifts from the Creator. These first bodies became known as "thought forms" according to the Edgar Cayce readings and were created by the souls without the sanction of the Creator. With the realization that they could create without the Creator, souls took their first step toward their unintentional separation from their Creator. Although the souls enjoyed the use of their "thought forms," their actions made them feel guilty for feeling proud at creating something new, something out of their own imagination, something they did not co-create with the Creator.

Imagination is certainly the key word as the Edgar Cayce readings portrayed some of the "thought forms" the souls invented. Apparently, their first attempts at creating a physical form were awkward and resembled monstrosities. Some "thought forms" appeared with the trunks of trees for legs and branches for arms. Others mentioned in the readings (363-10) included satyrs, mermaids, unicorns, and Cyclops to name a few. Although it is typically believed that the Greeks and Romans invented these mythical creatures of half man, half beast to tell a story or make a point, it appears that these types of bodies may have actually existed in pre-recorded history. In fact, it might also be possible that the reptilian body types that Scott-Elliott described as Lemurian were simply one of these many "thought forms" that originated at this time.

Other sources substantiate the use of "thought forms". One of these is author Carol Chapman who reported in her book *When We Were Gods* that she saw herself as a "thought form" during one of her past life regressions. Furthermore, her regression work presents modern day humans with an understanding of how souls may have entangled themselves in the material world and eventually became trapped here.

While under hypnosis, Chapman learned that the original intent of her foray into the earth was for the purpose of exploration. She first saw herself as a light beam, playing and dancing upon undulating waves or vibrations that turned into colors, especially the color pink and its various blends such as blue, mauve, and purple. As she moved with the color vibrations, she recounted hearing music and feeling the beautiful tones pulsating within her light beam. As she moved closer to the earth, the musical vibrations lowered themselves and began to sound like a pipe-organ when the lowest bass notes were played. She admitted that her fondness for that deep sound attracted her to experience the new vibrations more fully.

Only too late did Chapman realize that as her soul advanced more deeply into the attraction of the earth's vibration, her light became dimmer, the colors she followed became dark and murky, and the musical vibrations trembled more intensely inside her consciousness. So engrossed in how wonderful she felt with the new vibrations that despite these warning signs, she chose to continue with the experience. Caught in earth's vibration, Chapman reported feeling trapped into earth's energy field by some dark force she could not see. She could not free herself to instantly return to the Creator as she always willed herself to do until this moment.

Chapman also wrote about evolving into a "thought form" and described herself as resembling a genie just floating out of a lamp. From the waist to the ground, she observed that her lower form was a swirl of smoke rather than two legs she expected to see. Her torso was amber in color and her upper-body was as transparent as her misty bottom half. As she viewed her "thought form" under hypnosis, she realized that her whole new physical body was not even a solid mass, just simply a wisp of smoke. Although Chapman admitted that her new experience felt wonderful and exciting, she quickly discovered that her event just separated her from her Creator.

This separation feeling Chapman described apparently not only stopped the souls from returning "home" but also kept them in this one particular universe ruled by a star now known as the Sun. Souls trapped in the energy of the earth were no longer citizens of the various universes with the ability to travel from one star system to another. Chapman further explained that it was not the creating and possessing a new body form that was considered the breach with the Creator but the feelings that accompanied it. Chapman records: "We [the souls] had made the mistake of separating ourselves from humility, thereby making us vulnerable to a dark force which imprisoned us in the physical." Leaving humility by the wayside, the souls committed the sin of pride as they placed their will above God's for the first time. They felt ashamed at being trapped and embarrassed to face the Creator without first atoning for their mistake.

Projection Technique – the Third Root Race

Unfortunately, atonement did not take a priority. The excitement of experiencing what the earth offered while in a "thought form" body occupied the trapped souls' attention completely for an extended period of time. Eventually, they found a new way to participate in the physical world by discovering they could "project" themselves into matter, into already existing bodies. Although the two methods overlapped for a while, eventually the use of "thought forms" stopped and projection became the preferred means of participating with their material surroundings. Regrettably, the new innovation brought chaos, for the only bodies available on earth to project themselves into were limited to animal forms.

The souls' observation of the mating practice among animals precipitated their interest. Here was a ritual the souls could not fully experience even in their "thought forms", especially since created as androgynous beings. That was not to say that they did not try. Returning to Chapman's memories while under regression, she described experimenting in this way: "I found myself to be a small cloud that caressed over and under and around this black form in the shape of a bear or ape almost on all fours. I flitted around him, enjoying the deep feelings vibrating through me. I moved like a wind over his back, between his legs, and along his arms and buttocks. I could feel a corresponding tremor from the beast. It was exciting, something I had never experienced before."

Projecting into animal bodies was not an ideal situation for the soul. Since the souls possessed one of the highest vibration rates in all of creation, projection demanded a lowering of those vibrations to push themselves comfortably into the animal bodies. Fortunately, not all the souls participated in the projection of spirit into physical flesh, but enough took part in this practice to cause alarm on the part of the Creator and other souls monitoring soul activity on planet earth. In addition, this soul involvement in animal life caused extensive set-backs on two fronts. First, the participating souls abandoned their own spiritual identity and their own evolution. Secondly, they also interfered with the development and evolutionary paths of the animal bodies. Dr. Callahan, anthropologist and author of *Our Origen and Destiny,* reiterated the Edgar Cayce readings when she wrote that humans projecting themselves into matter was a selfish act and done without respect or acknowledgement of the natural order already at work on the planet. The souls abused their capabilities in the worst way.

The set-back for the souls themselves happened because they lost complete contact with the Creator while in animal flesh when their higher frequency clashed with the denser vibrations of animal forms. Moreover, the longer the souls remained in their chosen body mass, the harder it became for them to push themselves in and out at will. Soon, too many of them found themselves totally imprisoned within their projected bodies. This entrapment caused such disorientation with the spiritual connection that even when the animal body died and the soul was able to leave, it was so bewildered that it immediately projected itself into the first available body it saw rather than remember it was supposed to return to its spiritual roots and the Creator.

While the trapped souls regarded the projection technique as adventurous and fun, the spiritual world observing these events considered it disastrous. From their perspective, the souls could not continue decreasing their higher vibration rates for long periods of time. Souls desperately needed to reverse their descent into matter and return to their original spiritual vibration rate before they became lost to the Creator forever.

Intervention and the Fourth Root Race

To halt further descent into matter, the Creator intervened by first introducing a new law to govern nature where only like beings could produce like beings, ending the capability on earth to mate between dissimilar species. Its second step was the decision to create a new creature from which humankind would evolve. Although chosen as most suitable, the newly created body structure was not immediately ready for soul habitation. The new body had to complete an evolutionary process itself to eventually become the Adamic body, the new body-type that ushered in the Fourth Root Race.

The Creator's goal was to offer the souls a body that enabled them to keep their spiritual awareness. The animal bodies the souls projected themselves into were not constructed to do that. To maintain their connection to the Creator, the body needed to stand in an upright position and equipped with a highly developed endocrine system, a series of ductless glands throughout the body that would eventually include the gonads, the adrenals, the thymus, the thyroid, the pineal, and the pituitary. The requirement to stand erectly was necessary to allow the energy to flow without any impediment through the endocrine system, something the body of an animal on four legs would not be able to offer. Upon entering the physical body, the soul would attach itself to the endocrine system that provided it with the ability to raise its spiritual energy to flow from the gonads to the pituitary gland where it would connect with the energy of the Creator. In this way, soul and body would work together to spiritualize both, raising their vibrations to be more attuned to the Creator and less attuned to the material world.

Although only mammals possess a true endocrine system, the

Edgar Cayce readings clearly emphasized that the Adamic body did not evolve from the apes (Edgar Cayce reading 3744-44). Dr. Callahan explains that evolution should not mean that humans descended from monkeys but that at one point, humans and apes might share a common ancestor. That common ancestor was probably a hominid that split to develop two distinct lines of beings, one of them human.

Somewhere prior to 300,000 B.C., the Creator might have selected the hominid line for the divine intervention and started its evolutionary process to provide the body type for the Fourth Root Race. As the selected hominid line went through its evolutionary stages, the souls were barred from projecting themselves into these bodies. According to actress and writer Shirley MacLaine in her book, *The Camino*, her guide, John, explained that the souls trapped in animal bodies were placed in a somewhat unconscious state where they retained their intelligence but not their spirituality. They were not aware of their Divine origin.

Eventually, the Creator allowed these semi-conscious souls to re-enter the earth plane using the pre-Adamic bodies. This allowed the souls to shape the eventual final outward appearance of a human being while simultaneously attempting a spiritual return to their divine state. Eventually, these redeemed souls in their Adamic bodies developed to the point of establishing the beginnings of community, complete with customs and traditions.

MacLaine relates that it was at this point that the entrance of the Fourth Root Race began, and with it, the cycle of reincarnation. The souls who separated themselves from their Creator by entering animal bodies had much work to do to cleanse themselves of this wrong step. With the reincarnation cycle, they received multiple lifetimes to redeem themselves, to consider themselves worthy enough to become companions to the Creator once more.

The Fourth Root Race physical bodies maintained the androgynous form of its Creator. Yet, the male and female forms that existed in the animal kingdom intrigued the souls. Therefore, they desired to experiment with their androgynous state to simulate what they observed in the animal kingdom. Although the separation of the soul would cause it to lose its perfect balance of male and female or yin and yang energies, the experimentation became more alluring than allowing their perfect state to continue. Although several metaphysical sources mention the separation of the sexes, only MacLaine shared the process in detail in her book, *The Camino.* Therefore, it seems as though the beginning of the Fourth Root Race contained three body types: an androgyne, a male, and a female. Eventually, the androgyne body-type disappeared.

MacLaine's Journey on the Camino

The Camino is a road across the northern part of Spain used to make a pilgrimage to atone for sins. Today, people can walk the Camino or The Way of Saint James as it is sometimes called across the entire length of Spain, or at least walk a portion of the road, just as pilgrims did in the Middle Ages. MacLaine elected to walk the route in its entirety and mostly without the support and comfort of companionship. She considered the trek to be both an adventure and a spiritual challenge.

Allowed to spend a lot of time alone with their own thoughts, MacLaine contemplated and meditated for hours during her pilgrimage. Her solitude and meditative experiences resulted in visions of her past lives, among them a life in Lemuria. She was also granted a review of events surrounding creation. What she reported concerning the souls coming down to earth is similar to the information just presented. The only exception is that her visions included a complete description of how the separation of male and female energies happened.

Dividing Into Male and Female Form

While in one of her visionary states, MacLaine received guidance in the form of an understanding that this desire to separate was a project that began in Lemuria when a Council of Elders emphasized the need to reorder spiritual priories. Apparently the need to re-emphasize spiritual matters came because the Atlanteans valued their technological successes over everything else. Their new accomplishments had them stroking their egos, believing themselves more superior than others. The intent of the separation of the sexes was to diminish this new sense of self before too many beings fell into the same pattern of thinking. MacLaine wrote that the final agreement for this project was reached by all, indicating that a democratic process was probably in place.

As a Lemurian with an androgynous body, MacLaine made an agreement with another soul to be a portal for it by creating a body for its use while in the earth plane. MacLaine reported that she was, therefore, pregnant when she traveled from Lemuria to Atlantis to undertake her separation. She wrote of how she was intuitively led to a crystal pyramid shaped building where she was greeted by two Lemurians and three extra-terrestrials, all with genetic expertise. Confirming her commitment to the physical separation of her body, MacLaine was ushered into a room permeating with a blue mist and a crystal tank filled with golden liquid. Atlanteans joined the elder committee of Lemurians and extra-terrestrials and all thanked her for the courage to be of spiritual service by undertaking such a physical transformation.

MacLaine submerged her entire body in the golden liquid while the Council of Elders sat in a lotus position facing a pair of perfectly carved, crystal life-sized male and female forms. MacLaine observed herself going into a deep meditative state while the council members elevated their vibrations to extremely high frequencies. As their light energy increased, each member sent their amazingly bright light in the form of energy from their third eye area of their foreheads directly to the crystal forms in front of them. MacLaine observed that when the beams of light connected on the crystals, the light then arced from them to her body in the tank.

As her body expanded, MacLaine reported feeling no pain, just the accelerating power the council vibrated to her. Suddenly, she felt a second spinal column developing down her back. Next, she noticed an increased heartbeat that eventually materialized a second heart followed by a duplication of each internal organ. She then felt a body to her left side and another to her right. The one on the left formed female breasts and accepted the female genitalia as the body on her right side took the flat, masculine chest and the male genitalia.

As a second head was formed, MacLaine wrote that she began to feel the loss of her identity. As her head began to divide itself in two, she saw herself losing her original features. However, when the head division was complete, her original facial features belonged to the newly formed male body while the newly formed female side of herself contained a brand new set of features. Moreover, the soul who was to originally occupy the body MacLaine planned to produce as an androgyne now occupied the female form that had manifested during her separation process.

Although the two bodies now appeared as completely formed, MacLaine saw that the male and female bodies were still joined at the ribs. Only after the rib separation occurred was the division judged complete by the participating elders. Although the physical separation seemed a simple and straight forward process, this phase was nothing compared to the painful mental adjustments these separated beings faced after their division. Feelings of isolation and loneliness were prevalent MacLaine reported. Chapman's memories of this timeframe explained as well that until this point, the androgynous beings only experienced sensitivity. Feeling emotions was not a part of their knowledge.

Therefore, the divided souls were not prepared to deal with the gamut of human emotions unleashed among them. It is not surprising to learn that the compatibility and harmony souls had always known began to deteriorate. Instead of deepening their spiritual ties to the Creator which the male and female division was supposed to accomplish, the souls were now seduced by the physical bodies they occupied. They became enamored with the development of the male and female persona and ego, moving still further away from their spiritual heritage.

Second Wave of Souls

Meanwhile, a second wave of souls entered the earth plane with the mission to help the newly evolved souls adjust to the Adamic body. Together, the two soul groups began the first human civilization called Lemuria. There was much celebrating over the occasion for there are a number of Edgar Cayce readings that mention how the morning stars rejoiced at the event of the beginning of adamic man (or the Fourth Root race). Edgar Cayce reading 1857-2 claims that ". . . the morning stars stand together as they announced the glory of the coming of man."

The Edgar Cayce readings contain information that all races for the Fourth Root Race were created at once and placed in different parts of the world. The white race was assigned to the Carpathian Mountains (Turkey), the yellow race in the Gobi (China), the black race in Nubia (Sudan), the brown race in the Andes Mountains (Lemuria), and the red race in Atlantis.

As far as outward physical appearances of the five races are concerned, the Edgar Cayce readings explain that from the moment the different races were placed in their designated geographical locations, their bodies began to take on the outward characteristics necessary to comfortably reside in their area of the world. In other words, the new body type adapted to its environment.

Like the Second and Third Root Races before them, the Fourth Root Race souls could enter and leave the physical body at will. Unlike the previous root races, however, one could say that the Fourth Root Race souls were "assigned" a body as they were tied to their physical bodies by a thin cord that was possible to sever when the physical body died or at the will of the soul. However, if a soul cut its own attachment to a physical body, it was considered a spiritual suicide, which the spiritual world frowned upon.

Whenever a soul temporarily left the physical body to enter the spiritual world, the physical body was left behind looking as though it had entered a meditative state. Entering a physical form demanded a reduced vibrational frequency from the soul. Many of them were uncomfortable to remain at a low frequency for any length of time. For this reason, Lemurians did not always use their bodies.

Beginning of Civilization

With the influx of the second wave of souls, the Lemurian civilization officially began in a high state of consciousness, maintaining a close connection to the Creator, and trying to learn to adapt to a physical body. The early Lemurians did not consider themselves as separate from one another and, therefore, maintained a group mind. Individual consciousness did not exist. Without a sense of "self", selfishness did not exist in their society. Without having to deal with the concept of selfishness, people at the start of the Lemurian society led idyllic lives in love, peace, and harmony with each other, the natural world around them, and their Creator. Modern man can hardly conceive of such an existence at the present time.

Maintaining that deep connection to the Creator on a daily basis gave Lemurians an edge on learning and wisdom. The Creator imparted the knowledge of the entire Universe to them upon their request. The occultists led by Scott-Elliott implied that the Lemurians were unintelligent beings because they did not possess a brain. Because of their constant connection to the Creator, the Lemurians did not need a mind. In any situation, Lemurians received guidance or answers to their questions immediately from the Creator. This connection occurred because of their higher consciousness. Moreover, it is highly probable that people of Lemuria did possess at least the equivalent of the right side of the modern day brain structure. In fact, credit for the evolution of the modern-day brain began with the Lemurian civilization as will be seen in chapter 6.

It was a long journey from the moment the Creator produced the souls to the establishment of the great civilization of Lemuria, the most spiritual civilization the world has ever seen according to the Edgar Cayce readings (877-26). In fact, from a spiritual standpoint, Lemurians reached a height no other civilization ever achieved. Atlanteans started with the same level of spirituality only to allow its deterioration as this civilization became enamored with technology and their inventions.

The passage of the soul from creation to its entanglement with different physical body-types occurred through choices the souls made along the way from "thought form" to "projection" and finally to the occupancy of an Adamic body. Those who began the Lemurian civilization tried very hard to maintain their higher consciousness existence, complete with a daily attachment to the Creator. When destruction threatened their homeland, they made strategic attempts to save the best of their civilization for use by future generations. The following pages contain the story of their lifestyle, their danger from aggressive Atlanteans, the climatic changes that culminated with the final demise of their beloved homeland, and their forced migration to other parts of the world.

THE GOLDEN AGE OF LEMURIA

Because of the passage of time since the world lost Lemuria, coupled with the lack of ancient records and discoveries of any bodily remains from that era, supplying an accurate description of the typical Lemurian body type or physical appearance remains a challenge. Researching the paranormal sources uncovers conflicting descriptions of body types that range from the Theosophists belief on the one hand that the Lemurian bodies resembled reptiles complete with scales to the romantic version describing Lemurians as tall, slender beings of white light who didn't just walk but regally glided from place to place. The Lemurians were probably completely neither of these. However, when placing these extreme views aside, several paranormal sources provided enough information of what Lemurians looked like to understand that the physical bodies underwent transitions over 200,000 years just as all earthly plants and animals did and continue to do.

Several sources agree that the first Lemurians were androgynous beings. In the chronology of creation outlined in the previous chapter, androgynous beings were the first kind of bodies used by souls as they mirrored the "as above, so below" concept. In other words, since the soul was androgynous, therefore, so was the first body type. Or as Shirley MacLaine succinctly described it in her book, *The Camino*, the androgynous body served as a reflection of the soul.

It might also be possible that not only the Lemurian physical appearance but also their lifestyle underwent transitions. As with all civilizations, there is a rise to glory, a golden period, followed by a demise of the civilization itself. A similar timeline probably occurred for the Lemurian civilization which went through a spiritual or golden age and with the passage of time, experienced a decline from their original, idyllic lifestyle. For this reason, the description of Lemurians and their lifestyles will begin with its high points in the golden age.

Appearance

The famous Lazarus, a disincarnate entity channeled through Jach Pursel since 1974, claimed that the Lemurian being seemed to resemble neither a male nor a female, while MacLaine in *The Camino* wrote that they resembled more the feminine aspects of the androgynous body. Author Lauren Thyme in her channeled book, *The Lemurian Way,* wrote that because of the perfect balance of the yin and yang energies, the Lemurian bodies appeared more androgynous and more feminine in appearance.

While in their androgynous state, the souls maintained a constant relationship with the Creator and possessed the capability to use their divine creative energy to shape and bend the body into any form they wished. Eventually the souls decided they should separate the androgynous form into two separate bodies of male and female. In *The Camino*, MacLaine's spiritual guide explained to her that there was more than one reason why the Creator sanctioned a separation of the sexes rather than keep Adam, also known as the Fourth Root race body type, androgynous. First, even though the Lemurians in their androgynous bodies exhibited a highly evolved spirituality, they apparently still concentrated too much on "self." Because they enjoyed a perfect balance between their yin and yang energies, they thus tended to occupy themselves only with serving their own needs.

At the same time, the Atlanteans on the other side of the globe not only preoccupied themselves with the serving of the self, but became more and more attracted to technology and materialism rather than focus their concentration on the Creator as the Lemurians did. It became the belief among the souls residing on earth that separating the male and female parts contained in the androgynous body would allow souls residing in Atlantis to reorder their spiritual priorities while souls residing in both Lemuria and Atlantis would turn from selfishness and learn to serve the needs of other entities instead. For example, the male needed to learn how to serve the requirements of the female which were very different than his own and vice versa. The challenge would then become a discovery of how to serve the hopes and necessities of others while still maintaining a highly spiritual frame of mind.

In hindsight, the division of the sexes experiment failed. Instead of including the Creator in these new forms, the souls turned into their identities as males and females, paying attention to emotional senses that cropped up after the split rather than furthering their spirituality. This shift in emphasis began an obsession to operate on a logical level rather than the sensual or intuitive levels. Thus, instead of deepening their attachment to the Creator, the souls developed a whole new ego structure which did not make use of their free will in a positive way. Eventually, living life on the purely physical level became more attractive than paying attention to the divine origin of their soul.

Once the Lemurian race underwent the separation of the sexes, there is a variety in the descriptions of their appearance. Wishar Cerve in his book, *Lemuria*, wrote that they measured approximately six feet tall and weighed in around one hundred and sixty to two hundred pounds. Their main foods included vegetables and fruit, especially the mango claimed MacLaine. Their diet proves that they were not hunters and did not explore the country side searching for game or animals to kill. This information corroborates what the scientific community concluded to be the human lifestyle of those living in warmer climates at this particular time in history which was explained in Chapter 2.

MacLaine described the Lemurian as nearly seven feet tall with golden-orange skin and violet eyes. Although she detailed the appearance of only one Lemurian approaching her, she reported that his hair was blond and that no body hair was visible on any part of his anatomy including his face. Moreover, she highlighted the fact that the approaching Lemurian did not walk, but rather glided towards her. Although she observed that he wore sandals, his feet did not touch the ground.

Thyme described the Lemurian body as tall and slender with a dark complexion, dark eyes, and black hair. This description seems to be in sync with modern thinking of what people of the "brown" race should resemble – dark skin and dark hair. Since the Cayce readings stated that the brown pigment of the Fourth Root race was situated in Lemuria, his readings received a possible corroboration with this description. Moreover, bringing the present Polynesian people to mind, a generic description of the race would be brown skin and dark hair. Since these people might be Lemurian descendants, the similarity in physical descriptions between the present and the past should not be surprising.

Although the first adamic bodies in Lemuria resembled modern man in most respects, some slight differences in the very early Lemurians did exist. For instance, the human bodies exhibited more flexibility, for the Lemurian bodies were not quite as "hardened" or dense as bodies of today. This suppleness allowed the Lemurian soul to easily enter and leave the body at will, an activity Lemurians often executed.

Cerve reports that the body had extra appendages at that time such as six fingers and six toes instead of five. The Cayce readings attest to the fact that the human body once had the ability to manifest extra appendages as Edgar Cayce reading 877-26 explains: "Hardly could it be said that they were in the exact form as in the present. For there were more of the influences that might be used when necessary; such as arms or limbs, or feet or whatnot." The reading implies that the human body could add extra arms or legs when necessary. However, it is not clear whether or not the extra appendages, added whenever needed, were retractable.

Cerve documented that the heel of the Lemurian body included an extra protrusion behind the foot as well as webbing between the toes. The heel protrusion and the webbing might be logical appendages because the earth was not as solid or hard as it is today. It may have been difficult for humans to walk along the ground without sinking into it for a few inches. These extra appendages helped people's mobility at the time. In fact, the extra heel protrusion allowed the Lemurian to walk backward with as much ease as walking forward. Without the heel protrusion today, it is more difficult for a human to walk backward, especially in a straight line.

The Lemurians also possessed the ability to control the human body more than humans can today. For example, Cerve claimed that they could send increased strength to whatever parts of the body they needed to lift or move a heavy object. They could elevate or decrease their body temperature at will, depending on the outside temperature. How convenient this human capability would be today when disagreements arise as to where to set the thermostats to please everyone.

Cerve also wrote about a protrusion on the forehead of the Lemurians. Edgar Cayce reading 364-11 called this protrusion an extra eye: "In this the physiognomy was that of a full head, with an extra EYE - as it were . . ." Whether it is called a protrusion or the third eye, this extra organ served early humans in several ways. The most important function of this appendage was telepathic communication with the Creator and with each other.

Telepathic communication

The ancient Lemurians communicated with the Creator and with each other telepathically. During the Golden Age of this civilization, language did not exist according to the Austrian philosopher, Rudolf Steiner. Instead, the Lemurians kept in constant telepathic communication with the Creator for guidance and information. They were rarely out of the flow of this connection throughout their existence here on earth.

MacLaine described telepathy in clearer detail for modern man in *The Camino*. She reported that this method of communication was a language involving both the human emotion and imagination. Since she wasn't used to communicating telepathically, she claimed to visualize the words in her mind first. Then she concentrated on the emotions behind the words. Both the emotions and the visual image in her mind then projected themselves to the mind of the intended recipient.

For modern man, language would seem to be a quicker way to communicate. However, any beings easily exercising telepathy to interact can impress an image to others in an instant. That flash of communication is much quicker than trying to utter a sentence or string of sentences necessary to get a message across to someone else.

Since the use of language does not oftentimes appropriately convey the emotions and feelings behind words, additional sentences are needed to convey all feelings to make sure that the content of the message is not misinterpreted. While it is true that non-verbal cues and physical demeanor can help communicate the feelings behind the message, even these gestures can be misinterpreted.

According to Thyme, the Lemurians preferred telepathy over language even when other civilizations, namely the Atlanteans, began using language exclusively. The Lemurians felt a more complete and intimate connection with another being using their process of mind-reading. They felt that this method of communication did not allow any secrets to stand between humans. Thus, it also eliminated anyone's ability to lie. In fact, Thyme reported that the Lemurians felt uncomfortable with visitors who talked too much. Because they mistrusted the use of language, they looked upon information imparted through just the use of language as possibly untrue or even inaccurate.

The Lemurians became quite skillful with their telepathic capabilities. With practice, they could communicate with humans in other Lemurian communities even though the distance could be hundreds of miles away.

Without the sound of the human voice intruding in the atmosphere, Lemurians could more clearly hear the sounds of nature such as birds singing, water rushing around rocks in streams, and the wind rustling through the leaves. It is no wonder then that most of the paranormal sources all report how harmoniously the Lemurians felt with nature including the animals during their early or Golden Spiritual years. In fact, MacLaine expressed it best when she wrote that she could feel herself telepathically exchange thoughts with all of nature around her, especially the trees, flowers and the animals. She claimed she could even hear them respond to her attempts at communicating with them. MacLaine wrote that some of the animals would interact with her by moving near enough to touch her or stand on their hind legs. Whichever way they responded to her telepathic messages, she claimed that they did indeed touch her heart.

Eventually, the use of language eroded Lemurian dependence on telepathy as their main form of communication. With decreased use, the protrusion or the third eye receded. In time, the third eye faded to what we know today as the pituitary gland. With less use of the third eye, psychic ability in humans which was so much a part of the early Lemurians also began to recede. Most people today are so intrigued with someone who has psychic ability not realizing that these abilities reside silently in everyone, ready for use anytime someone wants to practice going within to access intuition.

Communities

The Lemurians lived in groups called communities which was a copy of the organizational structure they brought with them from the spirit world. In fact, the Cayce readings often used the term "soul groups" to indicate a group of souls who existed together on the spiritual side of the universe and even reincarnated into the physical plane together. This unity of souls was mentioned in many of Edgar Cayce's readings such as 877-26: "Then we find the entity . . . was among the children of the Law of One; entering through the natural sources that had been considered in the period as the means of establishing a family. However, they were rather as a group than as an individual family."

Thyme provided channeled material corroborating the belief of the soul group concept by recognizing that the Lemurian consciousness was a "tribal consciousness." Even though they acknowledged and respected the different aptitudes, capabilities and skills of each individual member within the group, they still considered themselves a collection of individuals who worked, thought, and made decisions as one single group-mind or group-consciousness. There was no room or tolerance for "individualism" in Lemuria.

This group mentality extended to the belief that no individual owned anything. Everything was shared including land, homes, food, material possessions, children, and even each other. No one owned anyone else. This attitude of "sharing" eliminated such negative emotions as jealousy and envy. The abundance of unconditional love in the community discouraged any attempts at meanness or desire to hurt anything or anyone. Also, there was no sense of competition and the desire to be better than anyone else or own something special to lord it over everyone else. Pride was not an emotion that existed in a Lemurian community. They had no heroes. Everyone was considered equal.

The negative emotion of fear had no place in the community either. With their ability to telepathically communicate with animals, the Lemurians didn't fear animals even the ones who hunted and killed other animals for their food. Conversely, since Lemurians didn't kill animals for food, animals didn't fear them either. People at that time considered nature and animals to be as one, inseparable from themselves, and part of the same circle of life. According to Thyme, no animal was domesticated at this time although many animals chose to befriend humans and became companions. Some animals even slept in people's homes, walked alongside them if they traveled, and even participated in celebrations or rituals.

The number of people residing within a community was kept to a manageable size, although sources report different population numbers. Whenever a community's size increased beyond manageable amounts, people volunteered to move to a new site and construct a new community or village. According to Thyme, the total Lemurian population of all the communities together numbered between ten and sixty thousand. James Churchward, author of *The Lost Continent of Mu*, based his population estimate on the *Troano Manuscript* and the *Codex Cortesianus*, Mayan books found in the Yucatan now preserved in British museums. His population number for Lemuria stood at 64 million people.

Churchward's demographic numbers are close to those presented to MacLaine by her spiritual guide, John. He maintained that Lemuria was home to fifty million souls containing all the predominant races (brown, white, black, red, and yellow) plus two more – golden–orange skin with violet eyes and violet skin with violet eyes. There is no mention of these two races in any other source material. One explanation for the variety of population numbers may be the fact that Lemurians experienced a population explosion that Ruth Montgomery wrote about in her book, *The World Before*. Otherwise, there is no other explanation in any of the paranormal sources for this discrepancy in number of inhabitants.

Like the human form, the earth's body has its peaks or meridians through which energy flows. These energy fields are called ley lines or grids, world grids. Understanding the earth's energy fields, Lemurians always built their communities on a grid and thus dynamically linked all their communities through the earth's energy field. Moreover, the Lemurians built their communities near water as they believed water was sacred and acted as a spiritual conductor for them.

The Lemurians developed their first settlements along the ocean shores. When no more room on the seacoast existed, communities moved inland, but always on an energy grid and near a water source such as waterfalls, rivers, or streams. Montgomery's sources claimed that many Lemurians spent their time fishing and developed a great talent for navigating the open seas. In fact, that ability remains today among some people of the Polynesian culture as they exhibit uncanny navigating skills. They can find their way over great expanses of open-ocean using only their inherited knowledge of waves and stars to guide them with astonishing accuracy.

According to Thyme, the Lemurians built their homes simply. Construction consisted of thatched huts with no walls, exposing their homes to the fresh air with nature all around them. In fact, their housing seemed to express their philosophy of being one with nature. Everyone in the community pitched in to build the homes and decorate them with wind chimes of their own designs and flowers. Knowing that crystals transmitted and amplified energy, they used them as decorative pieces in people's homes and placed more along their footpaths and walkways. The simplicity of their home design made it uncomplicated to rebuild their community if and when it was destroyed by major storms.

"Free" seems to be the key word to describe Lemurian life within these communities. According to Thyme, people slept when they were tired, ate when they were hungry, and played when they wanted. The souls came into the world and entered their bodies knowing their skill sets and willingly approached their assigned tasks with passion. No one had an occupation forced upon them. Their daily work contributed to the welfare of their community and also fulfilled them as they considered their work as "play". Paying attention to the phases of the moon, the majority of the Lemurian work production occurred between the new and full moon.

At the full moon, the women gathered together to rejuvenate not only themselves, but each other. They spent many hours in close proximity to females only, nurtured each other, and honored all things feminine. Meanwhile, the men celebrated their masculinity and banded together to unify their male energies. The Lemurians called this the Moon Time and, during this time, the men cared for the younger children, providing food for everyone while the women sequestered themselves for their time of female unity. In fact, on the Polynesian Islands where the old traditions are still the norm, the men still do all the cooking for their community.

Plenty of festivities and occasions to celebrate supplemented the Lemurian lifestyle. During these events, they lit and danced around bonfires, chanted, and ate a special food such as cooked beetles, the only food the Lemurians actually cooked according to Thyme. The beetle broth was believed to be an effective drink to help uplift them to their higher vibrations. Otherwise, their daily foods consisted of the abundant fruits, vegetables, herbs, and berries harvested from their natural environment. Actually, according to MacLaine, their main staple was the mango which when digested properly helped the Lemurians with their telepathic projections.

It is not that the Lemurian people were always in the company of another member of their community related Thyme. They also valued moments of solitude and scheduled time to be by themselves after the full moon. At the full moon, everyone in the community would gather together to meditate. Then, the two weeks from full to new moon became a quiet time for individuals to be by themselves to rest, to meditate, and to be introspective. In fact, everyone greatly reduced their activities at this time to give individuals a period of several days for the necessary solitude.

People exchanges were commonplace both between communities and within a single community. Members of various communities took the time to visit with each other, and oftentimes even lived with people of another village for an extended length of time. Within their own communities, the Lemurians would exchange homes as well as sexual partners. Thyme related that because of the philosophy that no one owned anyone else, and that with mutual consent, people became intimate with whomever they chose. This intimate exchange was possible because of the lack of covetousness and desirability in their society. It is important to understand that the idea of a family was not a concept at this time in history. The family structure did not exist. Instead, Lemurians thought, lived, played, and worked as a group or a community. This way of living is very difficult for modern humans to understand.

Atlanteans and people visiting from other societies considered the Lemurians very promiscuous. In fact, this belief in lack of ownership of anyone and the free exchange of mates was still in existence in the 16th century when Captain Cooke found the Polynesian Islands. James Michener wrote in his book *Hawaii* that the sailors on that expedition found very friendly natives in the Pacific Islands. Unfortunately, these reports served to have the Europeans and Americans of the 17th and 18th century judge these people as pagans when on the contrary, the descendants of the Lemurian people maintained strong spiritual ties with the Creator.

Council of Elders

The Golden Spiritual age of Lemuria did not have a hierarchy of any kind, not even for governmental purposes. Everyone was equal. However, a group of people known as the Council of Elders did exist. People consulted them for individual, community, and inter-community matters upon request. This Council was the closest thing to "law" that existed in Lemuria.

Because of their love and desire for cooperation, disagreements in communities rarely happened. When disputes did occur, the Council of Elders listened to both parties and offered recommendations to restore harmony. People tended to defer to the decisions of the Elders because of their knowledge of universal laws, those unseen laws that govern human behavior on the earth plane such as karma or "you reap what you sow" for example. In actuality, the Council retained no jurisdiction or power over anyone. Holding a position on the council was considered just one of the several occupations necessary to maintain a smoothly run community.

The Elders consisted of a group of men and women chosen before birth to serve their community in this consulting or counseling capacity. Trained in Universal Laws and Wisdom, they demonstrated the capability of accessing and holding what Thyme called the Golden Light of the Creator for their communities. Newly appointed Elders apprenticed with current, more experienced Council members for years before taking on any sacred responsibility.

During their apprenticeship, the new Elders gained knowledge of what would be called astrology today. They were taught the intricate relationships and vibrations between the sun, moon, stars and planets, and how all of this celestial interaction and activity would affect the souls currently residing on the earth. Elders were also cognizant of and well-informed on how to protect the link between dimensions and the earth's vibrations with the rest of the universe.

Pregnancy and Birth

This section on pregnancy and birth is channeled entirely from Thyme in her book, *The Lemurian Way*. She wrote that to balance the demands individuals and communities made upon the environment for survival, the Lemurians during the golden years limited the number of people residing in their communities. Consequently, a baby's arrival happened very rarely. In fact, adding another member to the group was a community decision rather than the desire of any individual to have a baby. One method of birth control had Lemurians use their mental abilities to visualize the sperm dying before it could fertilize an egg. Another was experiencing sexual pleasure while in light bodies rendering the chances of uniting the male sperm with the female egg almost nil. Light bodies are higher vibrational forms of human bodies. Lemurians could elevate themselves to their light bodies at will.

Since the Lemurians did not remain in their physical bodies for any long periods of time, they were often contacted by other souls who hovered around them in the spiritual plane, hoping to be assigned a physical body. Whenever a Lemurian community decided to create another human body, the Council of Elders convened in their temple to study the gifts and personalities of these incarnate souls lingering around them, expressing their desire to come into the planet. If the community needed another healer, they selected a "healer" soul type. If they needed a musician, then a soul who loved to play an instrument was selected, and so on.

Thyme reported that the Council's final acceptance was not only based on the talents and abilities the soul would bring into the physical plane but also the soul's aptitude for total compatibility with the rest of the community it would enter to serve. Planetary influences, otherwise known today as the astrological vibrations a soul carries, greatly influenced the Council's final selection of an appropriate soul.

Once the Council of Elders made their choice as to which soul would incarnate, they turned their attention to the selection of which female member of their community would be the mother. Among the hundreds of females available, the Council narrowed the field to a dozen women by assessing their potential for compatibility and connection to that of the in-coming soul. To be a mother, the female needed to lower her own soul vibration to thoroughly enter into her body to experience a physical union with a male to produce the fetus, and remain in that lower state of vibration for the nine month gestation period. This decision was a major one to make not only because it was difficult to maintain a lower vibration but also because the selected female would remain isolated from the rest of the community until the baby was born. Lastly, the new mother needed to agree that she would willingly release her newborn to the care of the entire community, emotionally detaching herself from the role as the major caregiver for the child.

The Council of Elders and the mother-to-be went into seclusion for several days to meditate on the selection of suitable men to father the baby. The males were narrowed down to fifty or less and were selected regardless of whether or not they already had a mate. Without the emotions of jealousy and possessiveness in Lemuria, whether or not the mother-to-be or the potential fathers had mates did not matter in the selection process.

While the choice of prospective fathers took place, the community built a special house outside the village for the new mother-to-be. With her comfort in mind, builders selected the best views and the best building materials. Once construction was finished, no one was allowed inside the new structure to avoid contaminating the home with incorrect vibrations for either the mother, or the unborn child, or both. However, the villagers continued to share the joy of a new baby's arrival through their daily giving of gifts that included the hanging of soothing wind chimes on the trees outside the home; the gifting of crystals to adorn the space; the surrounding of mother and child with a constant stream of light by healers encircling the home outside; and the placement of beautiful bouquets of flowers in containers around the home by gardeners. Other members of the community participated in the support of this sacred event by supplying food and other necessities as well as emotional support to the impending fathers and the mother-to-be. Not only did the community support the mother through the nine months of pregnancy but also for two additional years after the birth.

The community relieved the men selected as potential fathers from their chores and responsibilities and gathered them together in a special house of their own. Here, members of the community helped them to maintain the highest of energies by massaging them and presenting them with special foods. Although the female instantly knew that her mating ritual had produced a child, the name of the father was never mentioned among the members of the community. The reason for this secrecy was to ensure the baby did not belong to the birth parents but to the community as a whole.

Once the mother-to-be became pregnant, she focused on remaining in a physical form and meditated to create a bond between herself and the in-coming soul. Physically, she concentrated on her health by eating a special diet and strengthening the body through walking and other exercise. People in the community supported her through this isolation period by submerging themselves into their own physical bodies to keep her company, by taking walks with her, massaging her, and doing anything she needed to be comfortable through this process. Midwives also came to stay with her for short periods to teach her the physical and mental exercises she could use during the birthing process.

The last trimester of the pregnancy began the bonding process between the unborn child and the rest of the community. During the last three months of pregnancy, the mother visited each community member's home to introduce the unborn child to the people who would surround him or her after birth. She also visited with the Council of Elders where in communion with the unborn child, a date and time were mutually selected for the physical birth. At the appointed time, a conch was blown to remind the community of the impending event.

As the time of birth drew near, the community created the birthing place which was out in the fresh air, a house without walls but with a thatched roof overhead. Underneath the roof, a large hole was dug in the ground and lined with tightly woven leaves from various plants so that the hole or "earthwomb" as it was called was water tight. Members of the community filled the small pond with sacred water, healing herbs, and fragrant flowers.

Finally the entire community gathered to witness the birth of the child. Alerted by the sound of the conch, community members placed themselves around the perimeter of the "earthwomb". Others in attendance included the animal friends who maintained energetic attachments to the people in the village, members of other communities who traveled for miles for the occasion, and the Council of Elders who had spiritually supported the mother through the pregnancy. After birth, Council Members physically supported the baby in the water, allowing him or her to float as long as judged necessary for the child to feel trust. Meanwhile, each community member welcomed the baby by touching the child and beaming energies of love.

After the baby's birth, the community burned the mother's specially built home to the ground and the woman returned to her own family. The entire community pitched in to nurture and care for the child while the Council of Elders meditated to energize the chakra centers of the baby's body. This ritual encouraged the soul to remain in its new physical body. Entering a physical manifestation was not a comfortable process for the soul who previously resided in the spiritual dimension, and Elders tried their utmost to make the transition into the physical body as smooth as possible.

Raising a Child

Because the addition of a child in the community was a rare occurrence, the Lemurians held children in high regard and valued them greatly. Knowing that children were not solidly connected to the body during the first two years of life, the newborn was always lovingly held by a member of the community. The child was never left alone for any reason and even slept in someone's lap. When a toddler wanted to crawl or begin to walk, the entire community encouraged those activities, but the child immediately returned to someone's lap to cuddle or sleep afterwards.

The Lemurians applied the utmost gentility in raising their children and loved them unconditionally. Infants were grounded to the earth and integrated with nature by being bathed in near-by waterfalls, streams, or rivers. Infants experienced gentle massages on a daily basis. And, of course, since they were always in someone's lap, they experienced a continual sense of love. Although the Council of Elders did not actively participate in the everyday parenting of a child, they frequently observed the child's well-being as they regarded themselves as protectors and guardians.

Knowing the astrological influences governing the child as well as the reasons for incarnating into the earth, the Council and community members carefully nurtured a child's innate talents and gifts. They guided the children towards the direction of their purpose for being on the earth and no one imposed any of their own personal aspirations on them at any time. In addition, even as toddlers, the children were taught how to communicate telepathically, to chant, sing, and dance at a very young age which allowed them to participate in community festivities.

Upon turning two, a ritual was performed where members of the community began to give the child fruit and other natural, solid foods to eat. From this moment, a child began to find his or her own food to eat when hungry. This change moved a child from the daily routine of constantly being held to a sense of self-responsibility, exploring his or her own inner wisdom, and taking care of his or her own needs, although parenting continued for many more years.

At this time, children attended the sacred Light Temples to learn Universal Laws. Some of their teachers came as storytellers to instruct about Lemurian history through the art of storytelling while others came to teach the children about nature and every living creature around them. Also included in their curriculum were instructions of how to sound like various animals such as birds, insects, whales, and dolphins to better communicate with them. Lastly, other instructors honed the children's telepathic skills to convey information at great distances while others encouraged the use of innate psychic abilities on a daily basis.

A sense of harmony was bred into the children as they observed daily life in their community, especially when they witnessed how each member contributed to the welfare of others through their talents and special gifts. The community nourished the children's sense of creativity by allowing them to learn new skills. Children were allowed to work alongside various crafts people and urged to experiment with their new skills.

Somewhere between the ages of seven and eleven, depending upon when a child was ready, the community performed a Rite of Passage for them. This ritual not only honored the children but declared their readiness to embark on their chosen life's work determined before conception. The selected vocation was always an occupation the soul was passionate about, so graduating from childhood into their work phase was a joyful passage. Children then continued their earth journey by accepting an assigned home with a Master Craftsman in the line of employment destiny dictated for them. This apprenticeship period could last anywhere from ten to twenty years.

The skills learned during this period would then be practiced throughout their long and fruitful lives. In this way, work was creative play among the Lemurians, something that was done because of their talents and because they were automatically drawn toward their particular activity. Boredom was not an image that ever entered their mind as their work was a part of who they were and gave them their sense of value to their community. In other words, work was their creative outlet as well as their identity.

Light Temples

Every Lemurian community built a Temple and made sure it was located on an energy vortex in the middle of the village. If the Temple could be built on an incline, an elevation such as a mound, or even a mountain top, so much the better. The foundation, designed in a six-point star mosaic pattern, was built with crystals and stones. Four wooden poles were anchored in the foundation, but the rest of the structure had no walls and no roof. According to Thyme, the Temple's poles were highly polished and carved with what the Lemurians considered their sacred symbols. Lavishly adorned, flowing pieces of cloth made by members of the community hung from these poles, gaily waving whenever breezes blew through the Temple area. Churchward maintained that Lemurian temples used columns to indicate their entrances into sacred space. The columns probably replaced the wooden poles in time. Nevertheless, even with the passage of time, the Lemurian temples were still built without walls or roofs.

The reason for constructing Temples without a roof was to allow the sun to fall upon those meditating and worshipping the Creator, the source of their light. The roofless Temples allowed energy to flow unimpeded from the Creator to the people. MacLaine reported that upon entering a Lemurian Temple, she saw platforms upon which people could sit and meditate.

The Lemurians called their temples "Light Temples" because they became the portals for what they called the Golden Light which the Creator streamed to earth for their use claimed Thyme. That Light was the Lemurian lifeline to their Creator. It helped them receive Divine Wisdom and the unseen Universal Laws. The Golden Light was also instrumental to the removal of pain and rejuvenation of the physical bodies. The Atlanteans had their famous crystal for rejuvenation, while the Lemurians had their Golden Light.

Each Temple built in Lemuria held different energies and vibrations as well as purposes. Every Temple contained different instructions to learn different lessons or to gain different information. For this reason, it became imperative for the Council of Elders to travel from Temple to Temple as none were alike and needed to be experienced first-hand.

People came to the Temple to meditate. MacLaine's guide in Lemuria professed that meditation was done as a collective activity in the community to gain more electromagnetic energy as a group. Her guide, John, explained that communicating together was one element that helped them remain highly spiritually evolved. Being all of the same mind, the Lemurians endeavored to reach harmony for everyone in their community in order to maintain a peaceful existence.

Longevity

The Lemurians lived to be hundreds and even thousands of years old. There are three main reasons for this ability. First, they lived mainly in their light bodies and rarely used their physical bodies. Because it was a concentrated effort to lower their vibrations enough to enter their physical bodies, they utilized them only to eat, to eliminate, to create objects and other earth bound activities. Moreover, eating then did not mean three square meals a day as today's human body demands. Because the body in Lemurian times was not as dense as the human body is today, they could survive much as plants do, with light, air, and water. The Lemurians diligently followed the promptings from their bodies and ate only when they were hungry. Since being hungry did not happen daily as the physical body was not utilized very much during the course of a day, the Lemurian body lasted longer than today's human body.

A second reason for the long life span is that the Lemurians were still a part of a group mind and remained in this group thought rather than living and thinking for oneself alone. Surrounded by unconditional love, they felt at peace all the time. Therefore, there were no egos, no worries, anxieties, or stresses in Lemurian life, all factors that age the human body in modern times. Moreover, their lifestyle also placed a high emphasis on fun and relaxation. If a Lemurian felt an urge to play, work was dropped until that need was fulfilled. Today's society would not support such a philosophy!

Lastly, because death thoroughly severed the tie between the soul and its body, Lemurians had a tendency to remain with their assigned physical bodies for a long time. Once the decision to die and return to the spiritual realms was made, releasing the human body signaled a permanent break with the physical plane. The soul could not reverse the decision to let its body die. Once the physical contact with the earth was broken, a soul would oftentimes wait hundreds of years to return to earth as so many souls stood in line to be assigned a body. Therefore, the Lemurians held a "just in case" attitude and kept their attachment to their bodies for hundreds of years.

Women in Lemuria

Lemuria was a matriarchal society according to Edgar Cayce reading 630-2. The reading given to a woman who was told how in a past life in ancient times, she had taken a trip from Lemuria to what is now known as the state of Arizona, and learned that, "In that experience the entity was in the same sex as at present, but among those that were the leaders; for THEN the women RULED – rather than men." Ruth Montgomery's guides in *The World Before* maintained that the Lemurian community highly honored women because of their ability for reproduction, considered a co-creative ability, one that women shared with the Creator. This was considered the highest endorsement the Creator could bestow on his much loved souls, one given to the female and not the male.

Although the women took leadership roles, there was probably more equality between the male and female in Lemuria than at no other time in history. However, equality and respect are two different attributes. In addition to equality, the Lemurian women received the greatest respect within their communities because of their highly developed sense of intuition and their ability to bear children to continue human existence on earth.

Upon the separation of the sexes, both the Cayce readings and Rudolf Steiner mentioned how the female body received most of the intuitive capabilities that once existed entirely in the androgynous body. Edgar Cayce reading 262-20 claimed, "These become, as has been seen or given, in the feminine body more manifested than ordinarily in the male, in man forces, in that called intuition, or that which is active in that portion of the system." As the golden age began to slip and the ties to their Creator diminished, this intuitive capability moved the women in leadership positions as communities selected persons with the strongest intuition to lead them and impart guidance from the Creator. This is corroborated by Steiner who wrote that women exerted a great influence within their communities. Since they had been taught how to interpret nature, people went to them to seek advice or to translate signs seen in nature.

Steiner also explained how the intuitive and dreaming qualities were instilled into the females during their early years. As already mentioned in Chapter 2, little girls were placed outside during violent storms to calmly feel the natural power emitted by heavy winds, thunder, and lightening. Boys, on the other hand, had to undergo rigorous training in strength and bodily endurance. Perhaps the trials several Native American tribes traditionally put their boys through to achieve manhood are remnants or modifications of the tests the Lemurians once designed for their own male children.

Pockets of society still maintain matriarch societies today. David Hatcher Childress in his book *Lost Cities of China, Central Asia and India* found a tribe of people who still lived a matriarchal type of existence high up in the mountains of Pakistan. The group known as the Kafir Kailesh also remained true to an ancestral form of religion that includes ancestor worship, a byproduct of Lemurian social development. Some indigenous tribes of North America also conform to a matriarchal type of society including such Native American tribes as the Apache and Cherokee to name a few.

Over time, people change, communities change, civilizations change, and drastic earth climate modifications change people's environments as well. Atlanteans and humans from other civilizations came to make their home among the Lemurians, and negatively influenced their hosts' attitudes and views of the world. Add that to intense seismic activity contributing to drastic earth changes, and the main stimulus for the decrease of matriarchal societies in the ancient world can easily be understood. Almost overnight, the male's superior physical prowess became of utmost importance for survival during these severe earth changes, and for many societies, the ways and means of using intuition disappeared entirely. Learning to use intuition took second place to the urgency of finding food, water, and shelter to survive. Understandably, the matriarchal society needed to give way to more male influences which then ushered in the era of the patriarchal society.

CHAPTER

4

DECLINE OF THE GOLDEN ERA

Although Lemurians did travel within their homeland, they never wanted to leave the continent that nurtured their spiritual energy for even a short visit to other areas of the globe. The Lemurian elders, channeled through Lauren Thyme, claimed that if Lemurians left their sacred land, they were forced to lower their vibrations to remain in their physical bodies for the duration of their trip. With the lower vibrations, they could not connect with the spiritual energies as they did when they were home with full access to their Temples, the Council of Elders, members of their communities, and even the energy of the soil itself. Even their paths were strewn with crystals to support their higher consciousness if they chose to meditate as they walked.

The Lemurians claimed that if they left their country, they soon took on the energy of the land they traveled to. Therefore, without the Gold Light of their Temples, Lemurians could not regenerate their physical bodies which either died or became more dense or hardened. That shortened their life span considerably.

Were there other people to visit in other parts of the world during the Golden Age of Lemuria? Apparently, the answer to that question is "yes." Montgomery's guides wrote that there were other souls on earth who had been unproductive and missed several chances to maintain their higher consciousness even while they were still in spirit form. Although they had also obtained human bodies, these groups had isolated themselves in other parts of the world. Lacking social contact was detrimental to their mental growth, and the guides reported that these souls degenerated quickly. When they eventually came into contact with migrating Lemurians, they seemed behind in their traditions, conduct, and thought processes. Neanderthal man in the area of the world known as Europe today and the aborigines of Australia could very well have been some of the groups Montgomery's guides meant.

According to Thyme, each landmass on the earth had energy and vibrations unique unto itself. It's as though each different continent had its own thumb print that left its influence on the people living there. To be more precise, Thyme's information explains how important the earth's energy field was to humans as they influenced the energetic vibrations of human bodies as well as their group mindset, their attitudes and emotions, and spiritual progress. That knowledge alone illustrates how unique the land and the people of Lemuria must have seemed to the rest of the world. Their utopian existence sounds too good if not impossible to be true, especially to modern man.

Reasons for the Decline of the Golden Age

According to paranormal sources, there are four plausible reasons for the decline of the idyllic lifestyle the Lemurians created. The first is the status quo they adopted once they had progressed their existence to a state of perfection. The second reason is the erosion of Lemurian vibratory rates and attitudes as Atlanteans and other visitors inflicted negative influences upon their hosts when they made their homes on the continent of Lemuria. Thirdly, Thyme claimed that Altanteans detained Lemurian visitors and members of the Council of Elders in Atlantis unnecessarily, robbing the Lemurians of one of their important resources for the upkeep of their high spirituality. And lastly, the violent earth changes that drastically altered the geography of the world and brought unexpected changes, especially on the continent of Lemuria.

Maintaining the Status Quo

For tens of thousands of years, the Lemurians assimilated knowledge from the Creator on Universal laws through their Gold Light. Their Temples were full of knowledge which the Lemurians loved to share by turning their Temples into "universities." They improved their earthly living conditions, and mastered the maintenance of their group mind and their spirituality. Reaching a state of perfection, the Lemurians stopped expanding any further wrote Thyme. It was as though once reaching the state of perfection, they wanted to keep their civilization frozen in time.

While this tactic may have been a way to preserve their status quo, that decision did not serve them in the long run as outside influences eventually eroded the high levels of spirituality this civilization had achieved.

Atlanteans Discover Lemuria

As mentioned before, each land mass in the world had its own vibratory signature. The Atlanteans, residing on the other side of the globe from the Lemurians, absorbed a passionate, edgy kind of energy that led to a voracious inquisitiveness. That kind of energy led them to dabble into technology early into their civilization. They not only invented devices to make their lives easier, but they were eager to explore the unknown territories they knew existed beyond their own continent. Eventually they built ships and became skilled navigators which led them to the shores of the home-loving Lemurians. Although the Atlanteans judged the Lemurians as backwards and primitive because of their disinterest in technology, the Atlanteans instantly became intrigued with the body of knowledge the Lemurians were only too happy to share.

Like the Lemurians, the early Atlanteans were privy to the same spiritual connections and knowledge of the Universal Laws. However, they fell into the realm of complete materialism soon into their human experience, and according to Thyme, many felt the desire to control nature and each other long before they discovered the Lemurians.

Although the Atlanteans found the Lemurians to be childish and naïve, they were only too happy to amass the superior knowledge found in their Temples. To the Lemurians' chagrin, the Atlanteans absorbed their sophisticated information on sacred geometry, grids or ley lines, and vortexes along with the higher mathematics and other topics, only to use this advanced material for technical experimentation. The Lemurians were not enamored of new inventions or interested in absorbing them into their lifestyle mainly because they had absolutely no desire for change of any kind. Unfortunately, they learned too late that the Atlantean intention was not to use Lemurian knowledge for the betterment of all, but rather for selfish gain and power over people. The Atlanteans became masters in the art of manipulation, either through cunning or coercion.

At first, the Atlanteans came only to visit, trade, and learn the secrets of the universe from their Lemurian neighbors. Centuries later, the Atlanteans desired to colonize and build their homes there. The Council of Elders requested that the Atlanteans not build anything on the earth's energy grid lines. They were also requested to remain in their own colonies.

The first settlers abided by these requests, but eventually they began to encroach onto Lemurian sacred space, beguiling and manipulating the Council of Elders to tolerate their expansions. When the Council of Elders refused to give them permission to impinge upon Lemurian territory, the Council was ignored and the Atlanteans boldly began to spread themselves wherever they wished. Without a government to enforce the wishes of the Council coupled with the Lemurian desire for harmony, the Atlanteans had their way.

The first Lemurians to fall under the spell of those Atlanteans residing on their continent were the young people. Their simple communities and housing could not compare to the stunning cities the Atlanteans built there. The glamorous lifestyle was tempting to those too young to be thoroughly indoctrinated to the Lemurian way of life and thinking. It is rather ironic that it was Lemurian knowledge of higher mathematics and engineering that the Atlanteans adapted to build such impressive structures that lured the young Lemurians to the Atlantean culture.

Although the older Lemurians were irritated by the Atlantean habit of constantly talking without any sense of sincerity, the younger Lemurians found the constant chatter of the Atlanteans intriguing. It was the young Lemurians who broke the barrier of language versus telepathy by adapting to the Atlantean ways. Eventually, verbal conversation led to their loss of telepathy and intuitive sensitivity.

Appalled by the Lemurian attitude of sexual freedom and exchange of partners, Thyme's channeled material reported that the Atlanteans did manage to suspend their judgment of these "lower savages" long enough to participate in this free practice. With time, babies were born that were a blend of Lemurian and Atlantean heritage. This combined patrimony contributed to lowering the Lemurian vibration necessary to uphold their way of life. Some Lemurians even formally married Atlanteans and other visitors to their homeland, and left their continent to live with their partners elsewhere on the planet.

The Atlanteans even changed the palate of the younger Lemurians. They taught their new followers how to garden and domesticate animals that were later used for food. The older Lemurians were horrified at this new development. Their belief system did not advocate gardening but allowed the natural vegetation system to automatically produce what humans needed to eat. Moreover, the Lemurians honored plants and animals and telepathically communicated with them. The new physical activities of the young Lemurians changed their eating patterns, however, and they craved specific foods that older members in their communities just did not understand. Needless to say, these new eating habits contributed to denser bodies that then contributed to decreasing the higher vibrations the communities had once enjoyed.

Montgomery addresses this issue of new eating patterns when her guides revealed to her that some of the Lemurians continued to live frugally and ate sparingly. As time passed, these souls even shut themselves away from the rest of the world to be able to maintain some kind of vibratory connection to their Creator. They presented such sage advice and suggestions to the rest of the community that these people began to share their harvest with them. This exchange began the first priestly caste.

Honoring the Lemurian purists as priests and priestesses was an important step in the evolution of this ancient civilization. Until this time, all people, regardless of their occupation in the community, were considered equal. With the emergence of the priest/priestess came the beginnings of a caste system. For the first time, Lemuria experienced a governmental system as priest/priestesses' advice and decisions became law in their communities, especially when the Council of Elders became ineffective. In fact, the Atlanteans enlarged the role of this new caste system on their own continent of Atlantis.

Eventually, the Lemurians tried to protect themselves from total disintegration of their world by selecting the children who exhibited easy access to their sixth sense. Steiner claimed that to train the best of them eventually had to be done in isolation, therefore, those designated for extensive training were sent to special schools the Lemurians located and built in inner Asia. Here, they were able to remain pure and avoid the influence generated by the Atlanteans. This group came to be known as initiates. Some returned to their communities to serve as priests or priestesses. The best of the best remained behind to become teachers.

If Steiner's information is correct, the place in inner Asia where these initiates were schooled might be located in present-day Tibet. Although it is speculation, these special schools may have served as the foundations of Tibetan monasteries. If the Lemurians did begin mystery schools in Tibet, to find ancient manuscripts of Mu in secret libraries there enhances the odds that these records could be not only truly Lemurian in origin, but also the authentic sacred knowledge that this ancient civilization prized highly enough to keep it safe in a foreign land.

Lemurian Abductions

No other source except Thyme offers channeled material on Lemurian abductions by the Atlanteans. Apparently, the abductions began centuries after the two civilizations learned of each other's existence. Why some Atlanteans took unwilling Lemurians to Atlantis is not fully explained although the word "enslaved" was mentioned. According to Thyme, when Atlanteans seized Lemurians, they were not only taken to Atlantis but to colonies in Tibet, Egypt, the Middle East, parts of Europe, Africa, and South America.

Some of the enslaved Lemurians were used for scientific purposes.

Thyme wrote that Atlantean scientists experimented on the Lemurians in their efforts to learn how the Lemurian brain worked, how they could telepathically communicate with each other and how far, and how they could maintain and retrieve so much higher knowledge and information. The Atlanteans could never understand the Lemurian explanation that their knowledge and abilities were available to them through their direct connection to the Divine. That they needed the Golden Light from their Temples and the group mind of their communities to maintain the energy for this deep connection to the Creator, the source for all their learning and higher knowledge.

The members of the Council of Elders and the Lemurian Healers were found to be the best subjects for their testing and research. However, the loss of their Healers and especially their Elders took its toll on Lemuria as these were the people more highly trained to hold the Golden Light within the Temples. With the absence of their Elders, the Golden Light began to fade until, in time, it disappeared entirely. Temples, a place to meditate as a community as well as provide a center for the learning of higher consciousness, became dark. The final onslaught on the Temples happened when their fame became known to the rest of the world. They were then bombarded by outside visitors searching for a quick way to assimilate higher wisdom. Needless to say, the Temples did not survive this onslaught.

Earth Changes

In addition to holding together what was left of their once famous lifestyle, the Lemurians also became preoccupied with the rumblings of planet Earth. According to Montgomery, tectonic plates began to slide over one another and in some areas of the world, the earth's crust buckled. All this activity caused more earthquakes and other violent weather conditions. Winds became more frequent and stronger. Tsunami's washed out shorelines and communities. Volcanic eruptions along with other earth changes encouraged the rising of mountain ranges and contributed to the disappearance of lands to the bottom of oceans. The map of the world, if the Lemurians had one, was changing drastically by the year.

The earth changes also displaced large animals, such as mammoths, who threatened human life on the planet. Thyme wrote that between trying to survive the earth changes and the large animals, the Lemurians either migrated off their continent or began to live in caves or underground. Montgomery's guides documented that the large animal population presented such a danger in Lemuria that humans had to build mounds then dig cave-like rooms within these mounds to escape the destructive animal brutes who wanted to kill them.

Relying on Montgomery's documentation at this poignant time in Lemurian history, her guides recorded that the only souls who were safe from the destructive animals during this tumultuous era were the fishermen because there were not enough plants along the coastline to entice the large animals to the seacoast. Inland, women and children never left their mounds or underground homes. They lived in complete darkness with hardly any stimulation whatsoever.

Therefore, it was a significant occasion when the Atlanteans arrived in their first flying ship, landing on a lagoon in Lemuria wrote Montgomery's guides. Their appearance brought hope to the remaining population that once belonged to a highly spiritual and cultured civilization who had been degraded to live like animals, without purpose in their darkened mound-shaped homes.

The Atlantean plane, propelled and guided by the famous Atlantean crystal, was able to make it to the shores of Lemuria before the curvature of the earth would prohibit it to go any further as it would then have been out of reach of the crystal's power. Again, it is ironic to note that crystal knowledge came from the ancient Lemurians, but applied to technology by the Atlanteans. The spaceship landed on the beach, a safe location to be unmolested by the predatory animals. The Lemurians came out of their mounds and alerted other communities of the Atlantean visitors by using their wooden instruments. No longer using telepathy, the Lemurians broadcasted information from one village to the next for hundreds of miles through the use of drums.

The Atlanteans had come to gather Lemurian representation for an international conference to be held in Atlantis on the problem of these large animals that preyed upon humans throughout the world. Even the Cayce readings contained references to this famous meeting, which will be expanded upon in Chapter 7. Meanwhile, Montgomery's guides reported that the Lemurian elders gladly traveled to Atlantis to join other representatives who would gather from all over the world. Because the Atlanteans now had both boats and flying ships that could make the trip to Lemuria so easily, the guides added that some of the younger Lemurians were transported to Atlantis to learn engineering and chemical skills. This information from the guides certainly supported data taken from Thyme on the how and why the Lemurians left their homeland.

Marriage

Two people mating for life was not a Lemurian custom in the early years of the civilization. However, after the separation of the sexes, MacLaine noted that the Council of Elders began to recommend a monogamous marriage as they deemed it necessary for spiritual growth. She provided further details when she wrote in *The Camino* that the sexual division provoked a need for people to find their counterpart, the original androgynous half of themselves. That would be the only way to return to their original divine form. Although humanity would feel the aftereffects of the sexual division through eternity, the struggle to find their original half was necessary to make at-one-ment which would allow them to return within the grace of their Creator.

Although this viewpoint helps to explain why the institution of marriage became a part of the Lemurian lifestyle, the fact that marriage became recognized and incorporated into the Lemurian life at all was quite a step for them. Marriage seemed so contrary to their perspective because of their philosophy of non-ownership and sharing. However, leave it to the creative Lemurians to put a twist on this tradition.

Cerve is the only source available on the Lemurian marriage ritual. He writes that when a man and a woman found sufficient interest in each other to unite, they first went to their community leader, which was probably a priest or priestess, to record their intent. The leader then consulted with relatives and if there were no objections to the union, a date was set. At this appointed time, the young couple along with their relatives, and anyone else in the community who wished to attend, would gather in front of the temple. There, the young couple were undressed and a festive joyous procession accompanied them to the edge of the community where unoccupied land began.

The spiritual leader then asked for a piece of metal from both the male and the female. This request needed to be responded to with a "no" answer as it was a test to ensure that nothing had been concealed in their hair to bring with them into the unknown parts outside their community. The couple was then instructed by the spiritual leader to go into the wilderness for two months (two moon cycles).

When they returned, both the male and the female had to appear fully clothed and well-nourished. The woman had to show she had been comfortably provided for during this time. The male had to attest that the young woman had been a helpmate through this trial process. The couple reconfirmed that they wanted to be together and a date was then set for the official ceremony to take place. If the couple returned from their two month ordeal very unhappy with one another's company, no union between the two would take place. Moreover, the couple was banned from petitioning to unite with each other again. The decision made after the couple's return from living outside their community was irrevocable. Cerve explained that this "union" process is still observed in some of the cultures inhabiting the Pacific islands.

Death

As the destruction of the ancient Lemurian lifestyle continued, many of their ceremonies were changed or eliminated. Even their method of transitioning to the unseen realms through death underwent some moderate changes.

Lemurians did not die of disease. They maintained a healthy, balanced lifestyle with constant joy and lack of stress in their lives. Their healers invigorated their bodies before any illness struck using a combination of herbs, plants, crystals, and of course, the Golden Light. For injuries, the Healers were knowledgeable in psychic surgery and spiritual healing wrote Thyme. For this reason, Lemurians were able to choose when they wanted to leave their bodies permanently, a state called death.

Because they were familiar with reincarnation and so closely connected to the unseen realms, the Lemurians did not fear death but recognized it as a valued transition into another existence, one without the restraints of a physical body. Therefore, death was decided upon without fear of any kind.

Leaving the body was a major decision to make at this time. Once the soul left the body and severed the cord connecting the two, the separation was permanent. Moreover, once death was experienced, the soul was not able to reincarnate in Lemuria. The soul could return to earth only in another part of the world as there were too many entities already waiting for bodies to reside in Lemuria.

During the Golden Age of Lemuria, the soul would intuit that it was time for transition. Leaving the earth plane to avoid unfinished business or unpleasantness was strictly forbidden. Therefore, a discussion between the intended departed and the community centered on a review of the reasons for which the soul had entered the earth plane. The departing soul had to prove the intended mission had been fulfilled, that nothing had been left incomplete. The soul then consulted with the Council of Elders who studied their astrology to find the best time and date for the transition to occur.

Death rituals always occurred in the Temple after a community celebration since transitions were considered a joyful occasion. Oftentimes, members of other communities came, sometimes traveling hundreds of miles to participate in this commemorative event.

At the appointed time of the transition, the individual entered the Temple and laid in its center on the ground. The person was surrounded by crystals, healers, and the Council of Elders who held the Gold Light, asking the Creator for a smooth transition. The individual relaxed and within seconds, the soul left the body, an activity the person had done many times before. However, this time, the Council of Elders asked for the cord to be cut and molecularly dissolved the body.

After the Council of Elders ceased to exist and the Temples were closed to the Gold Light, the death ritual changed. The individual who wished to transition began the process by announcing to the community that he/she had made the decision to transcend in three days. Relatives and friends began preparations for transition while the individual settled all physical affairs. The Lemurians only had a few personal objects to give away at the time of their death as most everything in their lives was considered community property.

When all was ready, the Lemurian was brought to a selected burial place with ceremony. There the person would lie down with the head facing east, said appropriate last words to everyone present, and closed the eyes to enter a meditative state. It took a few hours to move the soul from the body as compared to just seconds during Lemuria's Golden Era. Relatives waited for three days, however, before sprinkling the body with a mineral of some sort to help it decay quickly without contaminating the soil. The body without the soul was not considered of importance anymore.

Over the years, the burial rites changed only slightly. Instead of laying down in the grave, the individual knelt or squatted facing east in their burial site with hands clasped in front of the body. The person making the transition meditated until the power of the will extracted the soul from the body. Some took hours and others took a day or more to transition the soul out of the body.

Whether during the Golden Era or later, there was no grief when a relative or a loved one transitioned from their present life. The living knew their connection would continue even without a physical presence. The closeness between loving relatives and friends of the departed member remained intact through telepathy. Links to those in the afterlife were discontinued only after the Lemurian civilization died out completely as there was not enough spirituality to continue the telepathic connections between the living and the dead. In addition, the loss of spirituality and hope the Lemurians maintained in the world soon allowed several negative emotions to crawl into mankind's psyche, one of which was the fear of death. In fact, humans still list the fear of death as the number one anxiety in their lives today.

Evaluating the Lemurian Age

Thyme, channeling the Elders of the Lemurian community, reported that the Elders believed their civilization failed on two fronts: 1) that they were so fearful of being in a physical body and losing their connection to the Creator that they completely failed to learn how to fully live in a physical body; and 2) that they were unable to raise the vibration of everyone on Earth to understand and access the Universal Wisdom.

The Lemurian civilization had certainly demanded lofty goals of themselves.

THE LEMURIAN PHILOSOPHY

According to the guides of author and journalist, Ruth Montgomery, the Lemurians were widely known for their philosophy in the ancient world. In spite of the Atlantean technical superiority, it is to their credit that they held the less-technologically inclined Lemurians in high esteem. According to Montgomery and the readings of Edgar Cayce, the Atlanteans exhibited a high reverence for the Lemurian Council of Elders and their spiritual philosophy which the Lemurians loved to share. Even after the Lemurian homeland disappeared under the Pacific Ocean, the Atlanteans continued to pay tribute to the Lemurians by venerating their philosophy until the worship of science, their greed, and their love of power superseded their worship of the Creator, resulting in the loss of respect for one another and nature.

Belief in Oneness

Belief in their one Creator or God and the Oneness of all things was the most fundamental principle underlying the Lemurean philosophy and the one that this civilization wanted to leave as their major legacy to the world. They understood that an energetic connection existed from one human being to another and between humans, plants, and animal life on the planet. Any action performed by one individual impacted everyone and everything else in the world. For this reason, the Lemurians did not consider themselves as individuals, but as part of a group. They thought as a group and worked as a group. Individuality just didn't exist. Separating oneself from other humans and nature was not a concept or a view of life even remotely considered by the ancient mind.

This belief in the oneness of all things is one of the reasons nature opened their essences to the Lemurians for their use. The Lemurians considered the essence or life force of an animal or plant as a part of themselves and as important as their own. The Lemurians never took anything from nature that nature wasn't willing to share with them. No plant life was ever destroyed and no animal was ever killed. In contrast, today's humans believe that their boundaries are their bodies, that they are separate from everyone else and definitely separate from animal and plant life. Modern humans believe that they are the masters of the universe which gives them the right not only to take whatever they want from nature, but destroy it at will.

Universal Law of Karma

Another legacy the Lemurians left behind is their knowledge of the Universal Law known as karma, which many believe is a concept that came from the Hindu religion of India. Although that assumption is correct, the knowledge of karma and its counterpoint, grace, came to India by way of Lemuria.

According to Shirley MacLaine's guide, the law of karma came into effect on earth even before Lemuria became a civilization. She explained how she was told that when the souls created what she called "useless" creatures such as the dinosaurs, the souls also began to argue among themselves. Eventually they did not even remember their own spiritual foundations and completely ignored the belief that any formation of new bodies ought to involve the Creator. As the souls continued to disregard their Creator's input as they conceived more weird and grotesque creatures, they simultaneously began manufacturing more negative energy, completely oblivious of actually doing so. Since no energy ever dies, the negative imbalance these original souls established would eventually find its way back to them. Thus, the law of karma came into effect as no one can sidestep the repercussion of either negative or positive energy.

The principle behind karma, or the law of cause and effect as it is called in the western world today, is that whatever energy or vibration humans put out in the Universe through either thought, word, action, or intent returns to them like the boomerang always returns to its sender. Karma is the return of negative thoughts or actions as well as the positive or harmonious energy humans might project.

Karma is an immutable law, whether people are aware of it or not. The Lemurians greatly respected this law of cause and effect, appreciating even the negative karma as they recognized that humans learned from mistakes. Whenever people in Lemuria complained of the "bad luck" that followed them, others reminded them that it was time to consciously examine their lives to identify the negative patterns in thought or action that attracted this streak of "bad luck" in the first place. According to Thyme in *The Lemurian Way*, the Lemurians believed that bad luck did not happen to anyone by chance.

To earn the high praise from Edgar Cayce's readings of being the most spiritual civilization of all time, the Lemurians intentionally and consistently practiced attracting positive patterns in their lives, embracing this universal law among others as a way of life. Their endeavors contributed to the harmony they maintained in their community. That harmony, in turn, assisted them in sustaining their high spiritual vibrations.

Gratitude

Expressing gratitude for what they had, what was provided, what they received, or what they learned evolved beyond a philosophy into a way of life for the Lemurians. Moreover, they expressed their gratitude for both the positive and the negative experiences, for again, they believed that the negative incidents often ushered in soul growth. According to Thyme, the Lemurians also recognized that whatever they focused on expanded in their lives. Therefore, they consciously chose to focus on gratitude for the good things that occurred to attract even more positive events to themselves.

Forgiveness

Forgiveness is another of the essential tools and philosophies that brought harmonious living conditions to a Lemurian community. The idea of forgiveness exists to exonerate those who hurt others, either physically, mentally, or emotionally. Whether or not the hurt is done consciously or unconsciously is irrelevant. A hurt puts out a negative pattern and karma goes into effect. In order to restore balance and attract grace back into one's life, forgiveness is the key to restoring that harmony. However, people often forget that forgiveness was and still is a two way street. The offender or perpetrator of the hurt must forgive himself or herself for performing the offence as well. In addition, the Lemurians believed that the person who was wronged needs to release and forgive the hurt and include any negative reaction expressed or exhibited on their part. Without the latter, the process of forgiveness is not complete.

Forgiving transgressions is an important universal truth to practice when living in a tightly knit community as the Lemurians did. Without the constant application of forgiveness, hurt festers, builds walls around people, and creates disharmony in community living. The Lemurian civilization would not have lasted as long as it did without the constant practice of this belief.

Truthful Communication

Another essential element necessary for harmonious community living is open and loving communication. Modern humans would call this honesty. To say something that does not match inner thoughts and emotions creates an uneasy feeling and even mistrust among the person or persons hearing the untruth according to Thyme who channeled this information from the Lemurian elders. Speaking the truth clears the energy and raises harmonious vibrations among the members of the group. Using loving communications also means to speak with the intention that what will be said is for everyone's highest good, not to deliberately hurt someone, and not for judgmental purposes or blame.

The Lemurian philosophy of loving communications also meant that no one attach a particular result to a conversation or negotiation, but to expect a win-win situation for all concerned. The philosophical Lemurian believed that if just one person won, then there were no wins at all. This belief stems from the high respect everyone exhibited for each other as no one was placed above or deemed more worthy than another in this ancient society.

Trust

The Lemurians believed that trust and surrender were basic philosophical principles that laid the groundwork for feeling safe on the earthplane. They trusted that the Creator truly loved them and took care of them while they lived on earth. Because of this belief, the Lemurians felt able to surrender and trust that whatever flowed in and out of their lives was meant to be. That it was unnecessary to control things or force the flow towards a predictable outcome. By accepting that everything was perfect and as it should be in their lives, fear-based emotions such as anger, envy, revenge, or hate did not have a place in their thought processes and, in fact, did not even exist within their range of emotions.

With the recognition that all was perfect in their universe, the acceptance of the safety of their surroundings transferred to an acceptance and trust of each other regardless of circumstances. Therefore, if someone in the community had a problem, the Lemurians considered it arrogant of anyone who wanted to come to the rescue and try to fix that person or that person's problem. Because they believed that consulting one's inner knowing or intuition was the way to solve whatever was causing disharmony at the moment, it was no one else's right in the community to even remotely pretend to know the answers for someone else.

According to Thyme, healers remained physically present at all times to help the person suffering from disharmony. They held positive energy around the sufferer until such time as he or she found a way to solve the dilemma. The healers' intention was simply to hold the energy open for an understanding to arrive either from the Creator or the person's intuitive self on how to shift the disharmony. Therefore, the Lemurian community allowed people to find their own solutions to their problems in their own perfect time. No one attempted to control or manipulate anyone while they sought ways to transform their disharmony. No one was ever told what to do or how to think.

Detachment

Not to take things personally was yet another philosophical principle that helped Lemurians live harmoniously in their communities. Thyme claimed that her resources called this ability, detachment. People in a Lemurian community recognized that everyone had a right to their own feelings, their own reactions, and their own truth. If someone said something that contradicted what others believed or thought, everyone knew that the statement came from that person's own wisdom and was not intended to harm or hurt anyone else. Therefore, no one took offense to what was said which eliminated the need to be defensive or argumentative which, in turn, ultimately leads to karmic repercussions.

The practice of detachment worked for the positive issues or events as well. If someone achieved an extraordinary deed or accomplishment of any kind, the process of detachment from their success allowed Lemurians to remain humble, knowing that all happens in perfect order. That belief coupled with the detachment to the success just experienced nullified any desire to become arrogant, proud, or self-centered. No one demanded glory or credit for good action. No one harbored the love of recognition.

Doing What They Loved

The Lemurians contributed to their community through their passion for certain activities and their creativity. In Chapter 3 on lifestyle, the Council of Elders and later the priests/priestesses of the community observed all Lemurian children from birth to determine what they loved to do. The children's penchant for certain activities was then directed to appropriate life work that satisfied their creativity and benefited the community at the same time. The Lemurians philosophized that creativity was a part of the soul and to spend a lifetime ignoring what one loved to do was to ignore one's higher purpose in life. That, metaphorically, "killed" the soul. The Lemurians knew that a lifetime full of creativity not only led to a life full of joy but also one of abundance.

Denial vs Willingness

In this modern society, "being in denial" is a term describing dishonesty with self or refusing to recognize the true intent of others. Denial was not in the Lemurian thought process or vocabulary. Instead, their thought process leaned towards "willingness." To the Lemurians, willingness was a sign of true wisdom, a possible conduit to miracles Lemurian elders told Thyme.

Humans in Lemuria were willing to take risks and make mistakes rather than not do anything at all. They were willing to learn something new, willing to be who they were, willing to be honest with themselves as well as with others, and the list goes on. The only brakes they applied to their willingness occurred when their intuition guided them to the contrary. They knew that going against their inner voices or intuition not only brought disharmony but also karmic consequences.

Non-Judgmental

Judging one another was not done in Lemuria. Their philosophical point was that no human could really know what resided in another human's heart unless that life was experienced completely. Since that was impossible to do, the Lemurians deemed that no judgment should ever be made upon another. Instead, they extended compassion to one another, a much healthier attitude than judgment.

Equality for All

That no one or nothing belonged to another was the underlying basis behind the Lemurian practice of unconditional love. The belief that every person and all things existed to benefit one another could not co-exist with the belief of ownership. Even when a male and female decided to make a commitment to reside with one another, the decision did not imply ownership of one individual to another.

Equality also extended itself within the community. No one was held in higher esteem than another. No job or occupation was considered more important than another. Although the members of the Council of Elders were held in high esteem, even the council members were not considered above anyone else. This belief in equality also made the practice of unconditional love an easier task for the Lemurians than it is today for modern humans.

Living in the Now

One factor that contributed to the ease with which the Lemurians lived their philosophy is that this civilization lived in the NOW, in the present moment. The past and the future did not exist for them, only the present. The left brain was not developed yet which means that they did not have an ego that constantly judged or a mind that maintained incessant chatter inside their heads. The beauty of living in the moment is re-introduced to modern humanity today through the work of Eckhart Tolle in his book, *The Power of Now*. He encourages humankind to leave the ego behind and become more connected to their essences, their hearts, and their souls in the present moment. After all, the past is done and the future depends on thoughts and actions of the present moment.

Living the Philosophy

In spite of Atlantean contribution to their downfall, the Lemurians lived their philosophy to the end as Thyme reports that they never blamed the Atlanteans for intruding onto their continent and into their lives. The disharmony and imbalance that caused the motherland's destruction can be traced to the Atlanteans' building their communities in Lemuria itself and although they were asked not to build on the same land energy lines or ley lines as the Lemurian communities, the Atlanteans did not honor the Lemurian request. Atlantean transgressions continued for years and included detaining members of the Council of Elders in Atlantis, swaying Lemurian youths away from the Lemurian way of life, and enticing many of them to even leave their homeland. Yet, the Lemurians never judged the Atlanteans on their conduct, never blamed them for the negative vibrations they brought, and continued to treat them as they would treat one of their own, with unconditional love.

Practicing all the threads of their philosophy together greatly contributed to the Lemurian ability to live their lives harmoniously as a group. In their world, no one experienced separation, loneliness, or abandonment. Existing in this constant state of grace took a little effort, but it allowed the Lemurian civilization to exist spiritually in peace and love for hundreds of thousands of years, until the Atlanteans arrived on their shores. It's almost as though this first ancient society knew the secret of living "as above, so below." They had brought heaven with them down to the earth plane.

CHAPTER

6

DEVELOPMENT OF THE HUMAN BRAIN

When dealing with the brain and the mind, a question arises whether both functions are one or two separate aspects of the human being. To clarify, the brain refers to the physical organ, while the mind involves consciousness, memory, judgment, and thinking abilities. Whether or not the mind is a part of the brain is still a topic of debate in scientific circles. However, as both the brain and the mind went through evolutionary changes from Lemurian times to the present, the additions made to both will be examined here.

As there are disagreements among the various sources concerning the physical appearance of the Lemurian people, so there is a diversity of thought as to whether or not their bodies contained a brain. It has already been noted in Chapter 1 that the Theosophists documented they did not.

However, according to the channeler Thyme, the souls who became known as Lemurians came to earth as soon as physical forms had evolved to the Homo sapiens stage. The Homo sapiens, the Fourth Root race body type of which the biblical Adam is an example, walked upright and contained a developed endocrine system, a circulatory and nervous system, and a brain.

Therefore, it is likely that the Lemurians did possess some form of a brain. If there were nervous and circulatory systems in their human body type, then there had to be a brain to automatically monitor those bodily functions as well as provide centralized control over the other organs of the body. Rudolf Steiner, a 20th century Austrian philosopher who read the Akashic Records (soul records), reported in his 1930's book on *Atlantis and Lemuria* that the physical brain and the mental capacities underwent an evolutionary process just as the physical bodies did. Therefore, the Lemurian brain did not resemble that of today's humans, and according to Steiner, did not have the same mental capabilities either.

The modern brain is an organ divided down the middle and comprised of two hemispheres, each performing different functions. The Lemurian brain, on the other hand, included only one of these hemispheres, what is known today as the right section of the modern brain. Whether or not the Lemurian right brain was larger than today's right hemisphere is not known.

As for the mind, it was minimally developed as compared to today's standards. According to Steiner's information, the very first Lemurians did not even possess a "memory" faculty as they practiced the art of just "being." They enjoyed what they were doing or looking at in the moment, and had no power to store the memory of the experience. Lemurians lived totally in the moment, in the present. The past and future did not exist for them, which makes sense as they were frequently out of their bodies and not completely living in "time" or third dimension.

The Lemurian minds were united with a higher consciousness where information was received for whatever they needed or wanted while residing on the earth plane. Perhaps Shirley MacLaine in *The Camino* explained it best when she wrote that the Lemurians realized that their ability to unite with the Creator gave them the most unquestionable and trustworthy source of information and knowledge. Translated to today's understanding of mind and consciousness, the Lemurians lived in a constant state of higher consciousness, known as the super-conscious mind in the Cayce readings or the collective unconscious according to Carl Jung, a Swiss psychologist. With no individuality, no subconscious mind or personal unconscious mind existed.

The Cayce readings contain an abundance of information on the mind where one learns that the modern mind consists of three sections or levels labelled as the conscious, the subconscious, and the super-conscious minds. Although using different terminology, Jung introduced the same concept early in the 20th century. Jung documented that the human psyche existed on three levels as well and called them the ego (the conscious mind), the personal unconscious and the collective unconscious. Jung believed the collective unconscious was a reservoir of all the experience and knowledge of the human species.

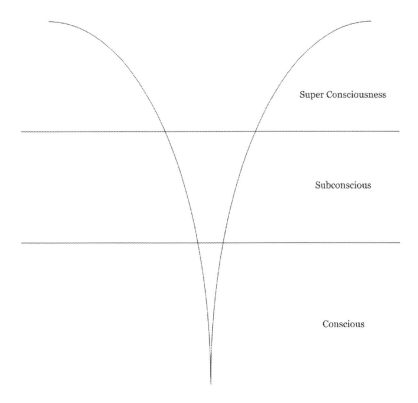

Illustration 1: According to the Edgar Cayce readings, every individual possesses three different mind levels labelled as the conscious, the subconscious, and the superconscious. The term superconscious and higher consciousness are interchangeable. Imagine the V in this illustration representing an individual person in possession of the three mind levels.

Jung's collective unconscious and Cayce's super-conscious are essentially the same thing although under different names. Both relate to the oneness of all: the Creator, plants, animals, and humans. As closely aligned as the two men are in their understanding of human consciousness, it is interesting to note that Cayce and Jung never met or corresponded with each other during their lifetimes.

Nevertheless, according to the Cayce readings, souls shared the super-conscious state with their Creator or God from the moment of creation. The super-conscious is the area of the mind where the concept of oneness prevails, where aligning individual will with that of the Creator, who is already higher consciousness, produces peace and harmony even while on earth.

This higher conscious state was the group mind the Lemurians shared which the Atlanteans just could not fully understand because they had already begun a deep separation from the Creator with their emphasis on the material and technological experimentations. Those interests contributed to their development of logical thought which began the growth of a left brain hemisphere and the subconscious mind development within each individual. They were removed from the ability of living only in the super-conscious state of the right brain.

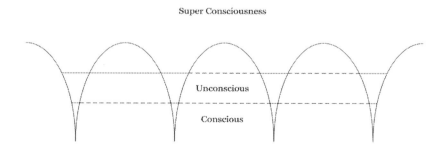

Illustration 2: If each V stands for an individual, one can see that at the superconscious level, everyone is connected. This is the "group" mind the Lemurians enjoyed and also illustrates the Oneness of all beings, the pivotal part of their philosophy.

Living in the Right Brain

What would it be like to live with only the right brain's capacity? Fortunately, that question can be answered today thanks to the work of Jill Bolte Taylor, Ph.D. Dr. Taylor is a neuroanatomist. She earned her Ph.D. from Indiana State University's department of Life Science program. In 1993, two years after receiving her degree, she moved to Boston to work in the Harvard Medical School Department of Psychiatry. Then, on December 10, 1996, Dr. Taylor suffered a debilitating stroke as she woke up that morning. It took her eight long years to recover.

What is different about Dr. Taylor's stroke from all others is that, being the trained scientist she is, she realized what was happening to her brain throughout the stroke, experiencing the shut-down of her left brain and its abilities along with it. She shared both what happened to her during the stroke and documented her observations throughout her recovery process in her 2008 book, *My Stroke of Insight*. What's of interest about her experience in this discussion is that with the damage done in her brain's left hemisphere, Dr. Taylor had access only to her right brain.

As blood permeated her left hemisphere, functions controlled by the left side of the brain diminished slowly before becoming inaccessible completely. Dr. Taylor reported that when her language center could no longer be accessed, she stopped recognizing words and didn't understand anything that was said to her. She could, however, feel the energy and emotion of the person talking to her which is a right brain function. She claimed she began to think in pictures rather than words. Her calculating skills also vanished to the point where she did not recognize numbers at all; in fact, she wrote that while living in her right brain, numbers looked like squiggles to her.

Dr. Taylor related how she became detached from memories and details about her life that her left brain once incessantly presented to her. With the disappearance of this constant brain chatter, she felt a calmness and peacefulness she had never known. Most importantly, she reported having a total connection to everyone and everything around her, feeling both fluid and at one with the entire universe.

Describing her experience of living in the right brain, Dr. Taylor wrote that she never felt in a rush to do anything. Calmly, she explained how she was able to shift from the thought of always having to do something, a message from her left brain, to just feeling content to be, a right brain message. She claimed that she didn't think or worry about the past or future because those cells in her brain were not functioning at the moment. All she could identify with was the here and now and she considered that a peaceful way to live.

Dr. Taylor's description of life in the right brain mirrors life for humans in Lemuria. The Lemurians lived in the present moment, peacefully connected to everything in the universe and to their Creator, communicating in pictures and feelings, and blissfully "being" in the flow with the world around them. The early Lemurians did not have a language, knew nothing of the past and future, and certainly could not identify with numbers.

To return to "normal" and participate in the world once more, Dr. Taylor knew she had to resurrect the mental abilities housed in her damaged left brain. One of the first cognitive functions she concentrated all of her energy on was memory. Curiously, Steiner claimed that memory was the first mental faculty added to the human mind during Lemurian times.

Memory and Language

Just how memory was added to the Lemurian brain Steiner does not explain. However, he conveyed that memory allowed the Lemurians to relate to objects outside of themselves and even give those objects names. Because of memory, whatever name they gave an object today could be remembered tomorrow and the day after that. The capacity to remember names given to objects eventually brought the onset of language. This ability to memorize also began the process of moving the Lemurian people from an "inner" life with a constant connection with the Creator to the ability to relate more fully to an "outside" world. The "inside" of humankind could now relate to objects and events "outside" of themselves.

At this time in human development, using the sound of the human voice was considered a very powerful and sacred act claimed Steiner and channeler Thyme. The Lemurians attributed the use of sound as an ability that came from the Creator. They believed that when sounds were used properly, blessings could come to its source. But if sound was used improperly, it could bring negative consequences to the person emanating that sound, again the karmic boomerang effect.

At first, the Lemurians used sound sparingly and only for specific purposes. For example, they learned at an early age how to reproduce animal sounds to summon the animals. Blowing a conch shell created a sound that notified people of an imminent, important event. The sounds of singing and chanting combined with musical instruments and drums inspired a higher vibration within the human body during times of meditation, rituals, and celebrations. The sounds of singing, chanting and toning were also utilized for the rejuvenation of bodies and for healing.

According to Thyme, the ancient Lemurians knew how to use sound to magically create any object out of nothing. They used sound to manipulate objects, from altering its size or denseness to actually dematerializing and rematerializing large objects such as stones and trees at will. On the negative side, they learned that sound could also be used for destruction.

The Lemurians recognized that certain sounds could annihilate an object, create an illness in someone, devastate another person's inner-harmony as well as destroy the compatibility between members of a community. Because of their spiritual philosophy and their knowledge of karma, however, using sound negatively was not practiced by the Lemurians, although the Atlantean usage of this dark side of sacred knowledge is another story.

Eventually, this intermittent use of sound became a language. The first attempts at language began as tonal inflections and had the Lemurians sounding as though they were singing claims Thyme. Their first words were simple ones, although they quickly learned that they could have a single word signify different meanings by varying its sound or its pitch. This use of one word changing its meaning by its pitch happens in the Chinese and Vietnamese languages of today.

The first words the Lemurians invented contained mostly vowels. The Cayce readings substantiated this, for whenever a person's name was given in a reading containing a Lemurian incarnation or lifetime, the letters were mostly vowels; for example, OUOWU in reading 691-1 and UULUOOA in reading 851-2. The current Hawaiian language is still composed mainly of vowels.

Besides creating a language, Lemurians also utilized memory to educate their children. Instead of giving them a set of rules to figure things out, the Lemurian children memorized the deeds and behaviors as performed by members of their communities. One would tend to call it today "memorizing the family business." When the Lemurians began to migrate to other lands, the people who left the motherland to begin a new community on another continent, carried with them the memory of how things were done from their old community. In this way, the Lemurians continued their ways of life even when they no longer resided on their beloved continent.

Adding the Subconscious Mind

With the advent of memory and language, the Lemurians began to separate themselves from their higher consciousness or their group mind. At first, the movement from their "inner" world to connect with objects and events in their "outer" world occurred only occasionally as they lived outside of their bodies so often. Eventually, the Lemurians remained in their physical bodies for longer periods of time and, consequently, began to frequently live in the outer world rather than in the group consciousness. Finally, this "outside the group" mind existence became a permanent pattern. Although they continued to maintain a connection to the higher consciousness especially through meditation, each individual also developed an additional mental level of their own which came to be called either the subconscious mind (Cayce) or the personal unconscious (Jung).

This mental development was a huge step towards another level of separation from their Creator and more individuation. As souls generated their own separate experiences during their physical lifetimes, the subconscious mind developed right alongside to retain the memory of their events and encounters. Therefore, over time, each individual's past lives, time between lives, along with the knowledge, proficiencies, beliefs, fears and other negative aspects learned in each material manifestation came to be not only stored in the Akashic Records but also in each person's subconscious mind. This section of the mind remains with the soul after the death of the physical body and moves on with each individual soul into his/her next earthly lifetime. This is also the mind level someone who practices hypnotherapy tries to have patients access during a past-life regression. Furthermore, it is considered by some metaphysical students to be the soul's mind – one that never dies.

The Downside of Memory

Memory brought further changes in Lemurian communities by creating a ruling hierarchy. At first, priests and priestesses, selected because of their exceptional intuitive abilities, served as leaders for their communities when the concept of a Council of Elders lost its effectiveness. Now, the leadership roles would make another shift.

Over time, the Lemurians expanded their memory ability not only to name items but also to remember outstanding and heroic events happening in their societies. Steiner claimed that people believed that those members who performed heroic deeds or exhibited outstanding behavior deserved recognition and rewards. Heroes arose and compensated for their gallant deeds by attaining leadership positions in their villages.

Some of these new rulers imposed laws and later, systems of government on their followers. Some also began to believe themselves to be better than anyone else and their leadership position was their due rather than an honor for services rendered to their fellow citizens. Others believed the leadership position should remain within their family, and succession and nepotism became the norm. Thus, self-aggrandizement was born and the days of equality in Lemuria ended.

According to Steiner, memory was also responsible for the development of ancestor worship, still practiced in some Asian countries such as China and Thailand. Families with heroic members began to honor these ancestors for their good deeds even after they were no longer on the physical plane. Stories of their heroic actions were passed down from generation to generation until they became more legendary than real. This remembrance began a pattern of continued veneration for ancestors, paying tribute to the departed rather than to the Creator.

Adding Conscious Mind or Ego

The last level added to the mind is the conscious or the ego. This section of the mind develops from lifetime to lifetime as the individual personality, influenced by heredity and environment. It is the "persona" humans present to interface in the world and its existence does not continue after death. This level of the mind began when ancient humans invented language along with judgment and logical thought which all contributed to the creation of the left brain or left hemisphere of the brain.

For the Lemurians, logical thought developed through necessity. Whenever problems arose as they migrated to different continents, the Lemurians had to "figure out" new ways of doing things if the environment barred them from performing tasks the way they had memorized. As new ways worked better, they would then put the new behavior in memory to pass along to the next generation. With the ability to remember both the new and the old ways of doing things came the ability to "judge" which one was better. With judgment came logical thought. Frequent use of logical thought became the norm and began the decline of the superb memory abilities.

With the Atlantean obsession of taking Lemurian sacred knowledge from their temples to invent new things, the Atlanteans boosted thinking capabilities to new heights. Their logical thinking processes knew no bounds when it came to "high technology." With the Atlantean advancement in logical thought, emphasis on meditation and the God-connection disappeared. They replaced the Creator with a false god called technology.

In reading the Akashic Records, Steiner explained that as additional capacities enhanced the mind, the body had to compensate for the new mental abilities with some loss of control over a part of the life force. One of the controls lost to the body was the ability to heighten adrenaline to increase strength in whatever part of the body they needed to lift or move something heavy. Humans could once direct the body to increase adrenaline to strengthen the arms or legs at will, which would then dissipate after the task was over. Today, adrenaline rushes are governed automatically by the body in response to an outside event.

Besides the loss of some control over the life force, logical thinking processes shifted another aspect in community life. Until this time, communities selected their leaders based on the memory of what an individual had done. Now, according to Steiner, leaders were selected on the basis of intelligence. This selection process brought out more negative characteristics exhibited by some rulers and tolerated by their subjects, characteristics such as ambition, selfishness, and the love of control – behavior far removed from the Lemurian philosophy and way of life.

Right Brain in the 21st Century

The right brain has not received much attention for centuries. Since the most sought after human skills of language, calculations, and logical thinking resided in the left hemisphere, even the scientific community believed that the right brain was not of much value. Many people today can remember how right-brain dominant children were penalized in elementary schools for writing with their left hand. Although it was well understood by the mid 1900's that the right brain dominated the left side of the body and the left brain dominated the right side of the body, teachers still insisted that right brain dominant children learn to write with their right hand instead of their left, negating their natural use of their right brain. Moreover, when right brain imaginative people were caught day-dreaming, they faced the accusation of wasting their time. Spending time using the imagination was not approved because it was judged unproductive. These are just small examples of how, until the late 20th century, the right brain was not considered equal to the left brain.

However, if the research of Daniel Pink is to be believed, the right brain is about to play a new role in the 21st century. In the 2006 edition of his book, *A Whole New Mind*, Pink explains how the world is moving from the Information Age to what he calls the Conceptual Age because of the three A's: abundance, Asia, and automation.

First, humanity has reached the stage of abundance with material goods, claims Pink. To differentiate its products, businesses will need to find a way to make their goods more beautiful or emotionally appealing over those of their competitors. An artist's touch will have to be applied to make products stand out in the marketplace and artistic ability is a function of the right brain.

The second A for Asia reminds us that people in that part of the world are now performing what large amounts of left-brain thinking, white-collar American workers use to do and the Asians are doing it at much lower salaries. Finally, automation, says Pink, is affecting white-collar workers of this generation in that many of the jobs they performed are now done by computers, robots, and other high tech innovations. They are suffering the same loss of work syndrome the blue-collar worker of yesterday went through when manufacturing jobs were shipped to other countries.

Pink predicts that the left brain thinking professionals now face the challenge of developing skills that computers cannot do and businesses cannot send to less-developed countries. Although the left brain skills will always be necessary, they are no longer enough. Such distinctive skills as pattern recognition, emotional context, artistic design, and seeing the big picture are the future requirements for workers in the 21st century. Those are right brain skills.

In the 21st century where high tech is no longer enough, the Lemurian right brain developed activities will see a comeback. Modern humans are recognizing that the right brain is not inferior, but provides a *different* way of looking at the world. It is today's task to blend the Lemurian right brain and the Atlantean left brain ways of thinking into a "whole new mind" as Pink calls it to move humankind into an exciting, yet uncharted, future.

DESTRUCTION OF THE LEMURIAN CONTINENT

Both scientific and paranormal sources agree that Lemuria's original land mass covered most of what is known today as the Pacific Ocean. By today's standards, this rather large area of land qualifies Lemuria to be considered a continent. Moreover, the name itself, *Lemuria*, is often synonymous with such phrases as "the lost continent" or "the lost civilization," and even "the lost continent of the Pacific." James Churchward nicknamed it the "motherland" and even "the motherland of Mu." His terms evoke an endearment for a once glorious civilization that declined rather drastically from a spiritual viewpoint, and never had the chance to make the necessary adjustments to rise again to its former glory. Instead, catastrophic earth changes ended its existence by destroying the land completely and submerging it to the bottom of the Pacific.

The world during Lemurian times did not resemble the world people see on a map or globe today. Earth changes throughout the ages constantly sent both small and large chunks of land plunging to the bottom of oceans while other pieces rose unexpectedly from the seas. Moreover, new land masses reclaimed from the oceans first needed to lose enough salt residue to allow vegetation to grow. Only then was the land considered or classified as habitable.

Lands also drifted as the surface is not anchored to the body or core of the earth. In fact, the results of continental drifts may often alter the shape of many continents by uniting one land mass with another to form a whole new look, only to have mother nature capriciously uncouple the joined lands millenniums later. Moreover, the north/south poles of the earth have also spun and shifted. Such an earth change as a pole shift drastically alters locations of lands and oceans. Therefore, the ancient world prior to recorded time was constantly in flux and underwent continual geographical changes.

Ancient Maps

Several early maps depicting the ancient Lemurian land do exist today, but cartographers question their authenticity. Are they really depicting antediluvian geography? Most maps of the ancient world provide no apparent proof of their origin. Fortunately, there are currently two popular Lemurian maps familiar to the experts of ancient mysteries. These were provided by creditable sources namely, Churchward and Cerve. Both writers claimed they found their maps in secret libraries in Asia. Churchward explains he found his map in a monastery library in India while Cerve wrote that he attained his map from the secret treasure troves of Tibet.

When comparing the two maps, one difference is immediately obvious. Churchward's map depicts Lemuria as an island, its outline encompassing most of the currently known Polynesian Islands (figure 1). In contrast, Cerve's map portrays Lemuria connected to the Asian continent as an extension of what is known today as China (figure 2). While both maps are strong possibilities for the shape of the Lemurian continent, the constant earth changes could account for the discrepancies. Therefore, the two maps of the Lemurian landscape might be providing views of the continent during different eras.

While both theories are possibilities, a stronger sense of the continent's position in regards to the rest of the world might benefit with some input from the Cayce readings since information from this source carries a high accuracy percentage.

Several readings offered verbal descriptions of ancient geography, not as a focal point of the intended information, but as an aside or an extended, unexpected explanation. With the Cayce readings in one hand and an adaptation of one of Cerve's map (figure 3) in the other, a more accurate picture can emerge of the earth at some point during Lemurian times.

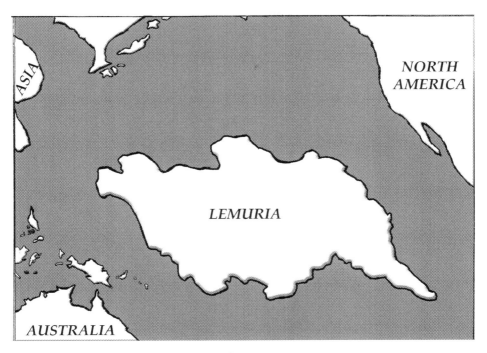

figure 1

Adapted by Rosemarie Marcotte   *Reprinted with permission. Adventures Unlimited Press*
                                                  From The Lost Continent of Mu by James Churchward)
James Churchward portrayed Lemuria as an island in the Pacific Ocean that encompassed most of the Polynesian Islands, including Easter Island.

Comparing the adapted map from Cerve's book (figure 2) with a modified map of the same area (figure 3), two differences become apparent: 1) in the modified map (figure 3), Lemurian borders reach further south and east, closer to the continents of North and South America; and 2) Atlantis appears more prominently on the other side of the thin strip of land that resembles prehistoric shapes of North and South America.

The changes were made, firstly, because the Cayce readings placed Atlantis in the current Sargasso Sea location which is right in the middle of the Atlantic Ocean. Consequently, the map in figure 3 positions Atlantis in the approximate area the readings indicated. However, the shape of the Atlantean continent is not known with any degree of certainty either from paranormal or scientific sources. Therefore, its shape is arbitrary. Secondly, the reason for drawing Lemuria further south than Cerve's map is because Cayce reading 364-13 reported that after the destruction, a section of the Lemurian continent merged with South America. Cerve's map seems to position Lemuria a little too high to the north for a piece of land to drift that far south – or perhaps not. One never knows with nature, and not enough research is available on the continental drifts to verify how easily land can move from north to south and vice versa. Consequently, this modification is a subjective one, a conjecture solely from the author's point of view.

Thirdly, a reason to draw the continents of Lemuria and North and South America so closely together is prompted by Montgomery's guides who claim that Lemuria's land mass stretched from northern portions of California to as far south as Peru in South America. The guides confirm that the continent then included the Pacific Islands known today as Hawaii, Tahiti, Polynesia, and Easter Island. They also revealed that today's state of California was once a part of Lemuria's eastern sea coast as well.

Turning to the Edgar Cayce readings 877-10 and 1256-1 where ancient lands are mentioned, the area of China and Tibet existed above water from early times, although the readings designated them as the Gobi. Currently, a desert, in northwestern China and southern Mongolia, is the only region where the name, Gobi, is still used. However, the readings claimed that this desert was once a thriving area of land with a lush, fertile landscape, filled with abundant vegetation to sustain the population living there.

Other parts of the world mentioned in the readings that might appear on ancient maps include the Carpathian Mountains of Turkey and the northern parts of Africa. At some point in time, the readings mentioned that Norway and Sweden were the only parts of Europe above water. Finally, looking at the Americas, the Cayce readings confirmed that the southwestern states of Arizona, New Mexico, Nevada, parts of Colorado and Idaho were above water in ancient times. Lands west of the Rockies and attached to the western side of the Rocky Mountains were not present on ancient maps just as the eastern seaboard of the United States did not surface until Atlantis submerged completely between 11,000 and 10,000 B.C.

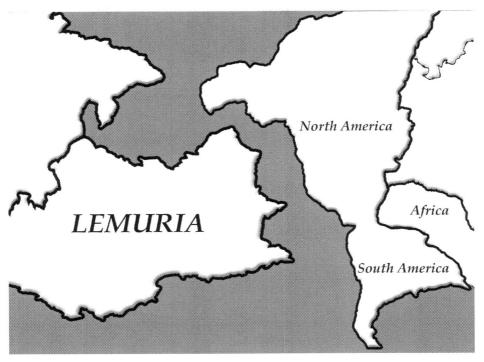

figure 2

Adapted by Rosemarie Marcotte   *Reprinted with permission. Rosicrucian Order, AMORC*
                                        From Lemuria, the Lost Continent of the Pacific by Wishar Cerve

Cerve's ancient map depicts the continent of Lemuria covering a large portion of the Pacific Ocean and an extension of what is known today as China.

Regarding South America, the only section of this continent mentioned in the readings was Peru, although it was referred to as Oz, not Peru and, unfortunately, with no additional information to satisfy a lover of ancient mysteries. Finally, the Andes Mountains did not configure as a part of the South American continent during Lemurian times, which gave that continent a narrower look on ancient maps. Therefore, the slim form of the Americas is a plausible depiction of the shape of those continents at that time, although those reduced outlines look quite unfamiliar to people today.

Why consider the Edgar Cayce readings as the optimal source for a world view of ancient times? Because recent discoveries provide proof of their historical accuracy. For example, the readings claimed that the Nile River coursed through the Sahara and emptied into the

Atlantic Ocean in earlier times. Once satellites were positioned in outer space, NASA data confirmed that the Nile indeed meandered through the Sahara Desert to flow into the Atlantic at some undetermined time in history. Further proof comes from Montgomery's guides who provided the information that a pole shift is responsible for the Nile's trajectory to the Mediterranean Sea instead of the Atlantic Ocean. Unfortunately, the guides did not give a timeframe for when this earth change occurred.

On a final note before leaving the maps: notice that the South American continent on this map (figure 3) divides into two sections. What is the Amazon jungle today appears as a large lake in ancient times. This was the probable waterway the Atlanteans traveled by boat to reach the Lemurian shorelines before the invention of the Atlantean air ships. Today, it is the speculation of several students of the Cayce readings that the Panama Canal happened because of the mass mind memory (or higher consciousness recall) that ships could reach the Pacific Ocean from the Atlantic without having to travel all the way around the entire South American continent - an interesting theory to consider.

Contributing Factors to Lemuria's Destruction

The instability of the Lemurian homeland began long before the continent disappeared to the bottom of the Pacific. In fact, a number of factors contributed to its final demise among which included a degradation of high spiritual vibrations and the proliferation of large animals creating a serious menace for humans.

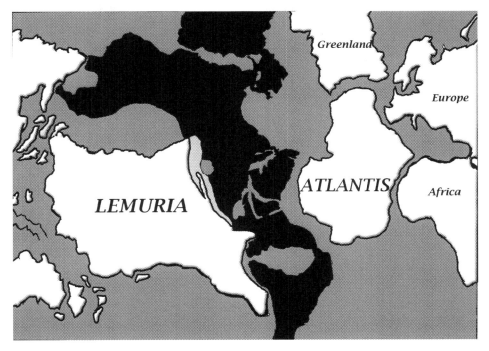

figure 3

Adapted by Rosemarie Marcotte   Reprinted with permission. Rosicrucian Order, AMORC
From Lemuria, the Lost Continent of the Pacific by Wishar Cerve

This map envisions an approximate world view of the ancient lands that were above water just before the disappearance of the continent of Lemuria.

Loss of the collective spirituality

The harmony of the collective mind that contributed to Lemuria's high levels of spirituality began to disappear when the Atlanteans arrived on their shores as explained in Chapter 4. The Atlantean tension and unrest eroded the harmonious energy projected by the Lemurians. Over the centuries, disharmony became the norm, and inequality along with feelings of Atlantean supremacy brought forth uncomfortable emotions between the two civilizations, stirring the dark momentum even further. Meditation times no longer provided enough power and strength to effectively restore peace and tranquility to boost Lemuria's energy field to the previous high levels. For these collective reasons, the human discord took its toll on the vibrations of the beloved homeland.

With the exception of the Lemurian civilization, what people didn't understand at that time, and what people still don't understand now, is the oneness of all life. Humans, plant-life, animals, and the Creator are all united with one another, all are one. Because of this energetic bond, human frequencies and attitudes gravely impact the earth's energy field and the nature it supports. When the Lemurian emotional balance became distorted, the magnetic frequencies of the earth where these humans resided became unbalanced.

The misaligned energies between the Lemurians and the land caused the earth to express its discomfort through earthquakes, volcanic eruptions, and tidal waves. With the loss of their collective spirituality, the positive vibrations emitting from the Lemurian people dwindled. Thus, they were no longer able to emanate enough energy to keep the continuing earth changes from weakening their continent. MacLaine explained that between astronomical movement, gravity pulls, and the disharmonious vibrations among people on earth, the continent was incapable of stabilizing itself and collapsed. She concluded that this was God's way to use the forces of nature to throw off and eradicate the disharmony and the damage done to nature by humanity.

Explosives and Large Animal Factor

As mentioned in chapter 4, the earth changes altered animal habitats enough for large animals to become a menace and a dangerous threat to the people residing on the earth at this time. Both the Cayce and Montgomery information used the term "large animals" which may lead to the assumption that the sources alluded to dinosaurs. It is important to point out, however, that the dinosaur era was long over. The large animal phenomenon during the time of Lemuria's existence entailed such prehistoric animals as mammoths, woolly mammoths, mastodons, and giant ground sloths to name a few.

Journalist Elizabeth Kolbert in her book *The Sixth Extinction* (2014) wrote of the first mastodon bones found in 1739 on the banks of the Ohio River not far from the present city of Cincinnati. They are now housed in Paris' Museum of Natural History. Charles le Moyne, the second Baron of Longueuil, and his French troops discovered a three and a half foot thigh bone, tusks, and a few molars the size of bricks, each weighing 10 pounds. Kolbert reported that the roots of those molars alone measured the length of a human hand. Although unknown to them as they pulled bone and molars from the mud of the Ohio, these French soldiers had uncovered the remains of an ancient mastodon.

From Kolbert's description alone, the size of the bone and molars leaves no doubt in anyone's mind that these "large animals" were tremendously enormous compared to a human being. Taking these dimensions into consideration, it is understandable why Lemurians ran away and hid in caves whenever these large beasts came near their communities. Humans possessed no weapons that would effectively defend themselves against animals of such enormous proportions at this time.

The Atlanteans began the world-wide crusade to rid the earth of these large animals by holding a summit, making it possible for representatives from all over the planet to attend by using their Atlantean inventions for transportation. Those included not only ships, but balloons, air ships controlled by the great Atlantean crystal, and what Edgar Cayce reading 262-39 indirectly referred to as zeppelins. This reading even provided a date for this memorable world meeting. It was 50,722 B.C.

At this first international meeting, the world leaders decided to flush out the young from their dens, to eliminate them before they became adults. Montgomery added that the technologically inclined Atlanteans invented a toxic gas that could be propelled into the animals' breeding grounds. To eradicate the adults, another device was invented to disturb their environments. Edgar Cayce reading 262-39 called this new innovation a Death Ray or a super-cosmic ray. According to Montgomery, this new device allowed humans to directly pursue the large animals rather than run and hide from them. With their weapons of destruction, humans bravely invaded the animals in their own lairs, something they could not do before the invention of these devastating tools.

Montgomery's guides wrote that the campaign against these huge animals lasted for hundreds of years. Several international meetings were held to discuss faster ways of ridding the world of this menace. Edgar Cayce reading 364-4 claimed that humans began to dabble in explosives to begin ". . . to cope with those of the beast form that OVERRAN the earth in many places." Three other Cayce readings refer to humans experimenting with explosives in Atlantis. For example, reading 621-1 for a young boy stated that he was ". . . among those who aided in the preparation of the explosives, or those things that set in motion the fires of the inner portions of the earth that were turned into destructive forces . . ."

Although the other two readings do not specifically state that the use of explosives were used to rid the earth of the large beasts, the descriptions of the experimentations with the explosives impress upon the reader the depth of the impact and disruption these destructive forces created upon the earth. Edgar Cayce Reading 820-1 claimed that people ". . . saw in those mighty upheavals from the destructive forces . . . the fires that were started for the fires of the deeper inferno that brought to the surface those destructive forces . . ." implying human capacity to influence drastic earth changes at will. Finally, the third and last Edgar Cayce reading, 877-26, claimed that ". . . the first of the upheavals; or the turning of the etheric rays' influence FROM the Sun . . ." produced an event similar to a volcanic upheaval.

These explosions, set off in all corners of the planet, occurred with the good intentions of ridding the population of the large beasts so humans could once again safely live on the earth without fear. However, the spiritual viewpoint was not considered in these decisions as humans negatively used the laws of nature. As a result, these explosions and use of destructive weapons weakened the electromagnetic forces of the earth not to mention causing volcanoes that raised mountain ranges, drastically changing the landscape and displacing humans from their homes, killing hundreds. Already out of balance and without the positive support of its human inhabitants, the Lemurian continent received a double dose of dissonance with these new deadly inventions.

Churchward and Gas Belts

Why did only Lemuria completely disappear and not any other civilization in other parts of the world? Churchward is the only Lemurian expert who offered an educated speculation, although during his lifetime, he was ridiculed for this theory. According to the geological information he gathered, he claimed that a series of gas chambers upheld the continent of Mu. When the chambers were emptied of their gases, the land above them fell into these chambers or gas pits, and the ocean rushed over the area once occupied by land.

Churchward claimed that in the *Troano Manuscript* and the *Codex Cortesianus* he found descriptions relating how the continent trembled and underwent a series of rolling or undulating land movements before it ruptured and dashed into pieces. Based on that description, Churchward concluded that a volcanic eruption could not have destroyed Lemuria as the land would have exploded into the air which did not match the accounts from the ancient manuscripts.

Although this is a rather simplified version of the calamity, Churchward's theories do have merit. The gas belts might have existed under the Pacific continent during Lemurian times. With explosions set all over the world to solve the large animal problem, the fires these detonations caused could have affected the gas belts or better still, the gas belts could have had its gas siphoned out and utilized to cause these eruptions. Although Churchward's arguments seem probable, it was never decided whether or not his conjectures had merit.

Final Destruction

The real reason for Lemuria's total demise is a natural cataclysm: a pole shift. Edgar Cayce reading 5249-1 stated that, "The entity then was among those who were of that group who gathered to rid the earth of the enormous animals which overran the earth, but ice, the entity found, nature, God, changed the poles and the animals were destroyed, though man attempted it in that activity of the meetings."

Montgomery's guides verified that a pole shift caused Lemuria's final demise. They wrote that the catastrophe began with volcanic explosions that sent tremors throughout the planet, and the earth shifted on its axis. The guides even supplied a date. It was approximately 48,000 B.C., nearly three thousand years after the initial world meeting that started this process.

The Lemurian continent disappeared overnight and over 64 million people died within a few short hours, wrote Churchward in his book *The Lost Continent of Mu*. MacLaine reported hearing millions of people calling out for help as volcanic activities beneath the surface of the continent triggered further disruptive upheavals. She saw the earth erupting, causing structures to topple and crush people as large ocean waves came crashing in at the same time.

Experiencing the emotions of terror and loneliness, MacLaine wrote that she elected to leave her body to float above the chaos although she did not immediately sever the cord tying her soul to her body. She expressed feelings of helplessness as she watched her fellow Lemurians being crushed to death or drowned as huge tidal waves displaced and covered the wounded land.

While chaos reigned, souls collectively began their ascent to the astral planes, leaving their physical bodies behind. These are the souls who chose to stay and die with their beloved continent. MacLaine compared the sinking continent to that of an aging dinosaur, unable to defend itself any further. She described a land that was abandoned by its human energy and devoid of the electromagnetic energy it had always counted upon to sustain itself. Although she experienced a very painful historical moment herself, she summarized the event best by putting her finger on the major impact of this calamity. She claimed that human spirituality had lost its home when Lemurian land ruptured and plunged under the sea. And indeed it did. Humans have never practiced or obtained this higher dimension of spirituality, this higher level of consciousness, since the demise of Lemuria.

Not all of Lemuria disappeared that fateful night, however. Thyme summarized that there are either physical remnants of a once great continent or the essence of its civilization in many places throughout the world. The land remnants included New Zealand, Australia, the Pacific Islands, Japan, and the western region of mainland United

States and Peru. On the positive side of this disastrous event, Thyme maintains that the Lemurian essence through its wisdom and lifestyle remained with those indigenous cultures who settled themselves on other continents to escape the disaster. She believes that Native Americans, the Australian Aborigines, Maoris of New Zealand, the Peruvian natives, Hawaiians, Tahitians, Samoans, and Tibetans are all descendants of this prerecorded civilization and still contain within their own societies remnants of the Lemurian culture.

However, the last chapter on the Lemurian homeland may yet to be written. The Edgar Cayce readings called the area around the Pacific Rim, the "Ring of Fire," and warned that the earth will continue to move, rumble, and change here. The 21st century has already experienced tsunamis triggered by underwater volcanic eruptions and earthquakes such as those that rocked Chile's shores and changed the Indonesian landscape and other shorelines bordering the Pacific Ocean. Who knows what nature will provide next? Perhaps one day, it might even decide to restore large sections if not the entire Lemurian continent to the surface of the Pacific. What a surprise to humankind that would be.

The Lemurian Migrations

Lemuria's total disappearance shocked the remaining world. No one expected the entire continent to be submerged almost overnight leaving only its mountaintops as evidence of its existence. Even the Atlanteans were stunned at the loss for they considered Lemuria to be the mother of civilization. The rest of the world felt distress as their prevalent belief was that only the Lemurians could keep the Atlantean aggression and ambition in check. When Lemuria vanished, their greatest fear struck and Atlantis established itself as the unquestionable leader of the world. However, according to Montgomery's guides, the Atlanteans were not as loved as the Lemurians because they blatantly flaunted their arrogance and their warlike tendencies.

Priests and priestesses of Lemuria warned the inhabitants of the Pacific continent several hundred years in advance that a catastrophe was approaching. Consequently, people were not obligated to leave Lemuria in a mad dash to escape imminent destruction. They had plenty of time to choose whether to migrate to other lands or stay to die with their homeland. At this time in their history, Lemurians chose not to leave their continent because the land's vibration supported them; therefore, migrating to other lands was a big decision and not one taken lightly. Those who left did so mainly to establish their lifestyle and wisdom in new territories so that their sacred knowledge would not be lost to future generations.

Because of the advanced warnings, the Lemurian colonists had plenty of time to establish themselves in other lands. They maintained constant contact with those who remained behind through telepathy and visits where transport to and from Lemuria took place by boat.

The term "motherland" probably evolved during this migration period as the main homeland of Lemuria nurtured her colonies by providing both physical, emotional, and spiritual support until the final demise of the Pacific continent.

In return, the migrating Lemurians, as well as their descendants, paid tribute to their origins by building temples to honor their homeland. In the Americas, the temples faced west towards the setting sun and in the direction of the motherland as prehistoric temples at Uxmal and elsewhere in Mexico face west. In Asia, the temples such as those at Angkor, Cambodia, faced east, acknowledging their heritage to Mu. According to Montgomery's guides, this method of honoring the motherland continued for thousands of years after the continent disappeared.

Asia

The Gobi

Since the Lemurians already educated their highly intuitive children in Asia, it is logical that this location attracted one of the first migration. The regions of China and Mongolia, known as The Gobi at this time, allowed the Lemurians to easily and quietly settle into the area. Staying to themselves at first, they eventually mixed with the yellow race, the original inhabitants of this land. Although the earliest occupants of the Gobi were not as spiritually advanced as the Lemurians, the new settlers found the natives to be a quiet and cultured type of people. According to Montgomery, because of their mutual love of philosophy, the Lemurians and yellow ethnic group developed "a race of Thinkers" here long before Lemuria disappeared.

Lemurian customs and lifestyles continued in the Gobi when priests and priestesses withdrew from the daily activities of the community as they did in their homeland. In their new surroundings, they established monasteries for their seclusion. After the pole shift raised the Himalayan mountain ranges, monasteries were transferred to the new mountaintops, allowing the priestly inhabitants to maintain a closer connection to the Creative forces higher up in the mountain terrain. Although the Montgomery guides attest that these monasteries endured for thousands of years, they are probably not in existence today. However, perhaps their books, records, and other paper collections are now the manuscripts from the "secret libraries" that the residents of these monasteries placed in hiding at some time in history to avoid vandalism.

The Edgar Cayce readings (873-1, 877-10) mentioned that residents of the Gobi built a Temple of Gold and eventually an entire City of Gold. Besides the gold overlay added to the Temple structure, the readings remarked that this area contained one of the first Temples where wood was used as building material. Edgar Cayce reading 877-10 further explained that the use of wood in this Temple went beyond the beams and walls to the use of panels containing ". . . many colored, polished woods." These various ways of using wood was apparently a first among the Lemurian descendants, otherwise the readings would not have mentioned such a detail.

Unfortunately, people's negative thoughts and behaviors eventually caused the destruction of the City of Gold, said the reading, and it was eventually bombarded by windstorms which buried it in sand. Tens of thousands of years later, this Golden City still waits to be found and excavated.

Indochina

Indochina is a section of land located southeast of mainland China. Today, it includes the countries of Vietnam, Cambodia, and Laos. A group of Lemurians settled a colony here during ancient times. Edgar Cayce reading 2067-1 noted that this new colony elected to continue a Lemurian tradition by selecting women as leaders and rulers in their new homeland, establishing a matriarchal society here.

The people flourished in their new environment and, finding that gold was plentiful, built a temple and a city of gold here as well. Whether or not their creation of another City of Gold was to imitate the one in the Gobi is not known. However, Edgar Cayce reading 1298-1 claimed that this golden city was eventually destroyed through illness caused by an insect, "For as man may find even in this day and generation, the insect becomes the defeater of man's purposes in many of his endeavors. For, because of those activities, there came upon the land that horde of those forces that brought to the peoples that DREAD activity in the body that EMPTIED the land of its peoples!" It is difficult to imagine a beautiful City of Gold, empty of people, a ghost town in the midst of such beauty and luxury. There is no further information on how the city itself was finally destroyed.

Two Asian civilizations created two cities of gold. Could these be the legendary eastern cities of gold which Westerners tried so hard to find? Could these cities be those that Columbus and the Spanish conquistadors expected to discover on their expeditions across the Atlantic and transferred their expectations of gold to the Americas instead?

India

Churchward was convinced that India was settled by the Lemurians and became one of the motherland's colonies. No one believed him as he did not offer any documented or archeological proof. However, Montgomery's guides verified several years later that the Lemurians did indeed establish a colony in India. In fact, it was the settlers' hope to form a second Lemurian culture here since the land had no previous inhabitants. Eventually, members of the Yellow race came down from the north to establish their own settlements near the Lemurians. They were soon joined by members of the Black and Aryan races too. However, the Lemurians, members of the Brown race, were the first to settle here.

Naturally, the races settling in ancient India eventually did intermarry. It is apparent that since all these races established their settlements near each other without conflict, it reflected a lack of concern with race issues or of keeping a race pure at this time in history. According to Montgomery's guides, the present day people of India are a blend of the brown (Lemurian), yellow, black, and white races.

In fact, the guides provided the information that the caste system in India was originally based upon the various races settling here.

First and highest were the Lemurian priests, followed by regular Lemurians, then the Yellow, Black, and White settlers along with the strata of society known in ancient times as "Things" who started the Untouchable layer of India's caste system.

"Things" were souls trapped in bodies that resembled humans but were cursed with animal appendages of some kind – such as wings for arms, or bird claws instead of hands, hooves instead of feet, tails, etc. They were used as beasts of burden in prerecorded times. The Edgar Cayce readings alluded to "Things" in many readings concerning Atlantis where it was also reported that they were not treated very well. Montgomery's guides claimed that "Things" eventually disappeared because the Atlanteans and an Egyptian priest surgically removed their appendages and controlled their breeding. Propagation between two former "Thing" beings was monitored until their descendants were born with less deformities or complete normality.

Middle East

The Lemurians migrated all the way to the section of the world known today as the Middle East. One group settled in the Mesopotamia area, on land between the Tigris and Euphrates Rivers where the white race was already established. According to Montgomery's guides, the Lemurians introduced cuneiform writing to the area and adamantly preserved the religious rites of the motherland, especially in the belief of the one God. It is suspected that they were the foundation of a civilization that became known as the Sumerians.

A second group of Lemurians wandered further north and west of the Mesopotamian area onto lands known as Syria and Israel today. Unlike all the other colonies, this Lemurian group was restless, claimed Montgomery's guides, and did not settle to farm the land. Instead, they became wandering nomads and raised large flocks of sheep they brought with them from the Gobi. Eventually mixing with the White race, they managed to hold onto their religious beliefs of the One God. This group of migrating Lemurians were the precursors of the Semitic race.

North America

American Southwest

While traveling through the American Southwest, Churchward found symbols carved on rocks and in cliff dwellings that he claimed had originated in Mu. Based on that evidence, he boldly declared that the Lemurians had settled here. Although he was accurate, no one else had ever seen those Mu symbols from the monastery tablets in India and that made his assertions difficult to believe at the time. However, several past life readings from Cayce along with material from Montgomery's guides have substantiated and upheld these Churchward insights. The Lemurians did indeed establish colonies in the southwestern parts of the United States.

Over 91 Cayce past-life readings mentioned that people had come from Lemuria, or experienced a lifetime there. A handful of readings even gave a few details on Lemurian settlements in the American southwest. Examining those Edgar Cayce readings, one person, 962-1, underwent a lifetime in America, specifically in the section of the United States known today as ". . . Arizona, New Mexico, [and] Colorado. There the entity was among those who were the outcome of those who had come from the land of Mu, or Lemuria." Edgar Cayce reading 691-1 reported that someone else was among the first to be born in America to Lemurians who had settled colonies there: "Before that we find the entity was in that land now known as the American, during the periods when there were the sojourning of those from the land of Mu, or Lemuria. The entity was then among the first of those that were born in what is now portions of Arizona and of Utah, and among those that established the lands there for the building up . . ." of another Lemurian civilization in a new land.

Edgar Cayce reading 851-2 listed many of the southwestern states the Lemurians colonized while taking refuge from their sinking continent: "Before that we find the entity was in that land now known as the American, during those periods when these were the changes that had brought about the sinking of Mu or Lemuria, or those peoples in the periods who had changed to what is now a portion of the Rocky

Mountain area, Arizona, New Mexico, portions of Nevada and Utah." Another Edgar Cayce reading, 509-1, reported that "Before this we find the entity in that land now known as the American, during the periods when the Lemurian or the lands of Mu or Zu were being in their turmoils for destruction. And the entity was among those that . . . established a temple of worship for those that escaped from the turmoils of the shifting of the earth at that particular period."

Extensive research on Indian tribes in the American Southwest led Churchward to conclude that the Pueblo Indian line in particular were of Lemurian descent. He explained that one of the proofs for this statement was that the Hopi and Zuni Indian tribes, segments of the Pueblo Indians, told a legend of their forefathers coming to America by ships from land located in the direction of the setting sun, which is, of course, a westerly direction. Lemuria certainly resided west of the Americas.

Another argument Churchward presented for his conclusion regarding the Indian tribes was that more than any other group in the southwest, the Hopi and Zuni had the same sacred symbols he had seen on tablets in India that the monks attributed to Mu origins. Moreover, Churchward wrote that the Hopi religious beliefs contained sophisticated thoughts that had to come from a higher civilization. For example, the Hopis believed that human beings were the children of God and not the offspring of nature. In Churchward's opinion, these were not beliefs normally associated with primitive people.

Further support that the Zuni were of Lemurian descent came from an unexpected source, a volume entitled *God, Gold and Glory* written by Nicholas Hordern. The author wrote that Spanish soldiers under the command of Francisco Vasquez de Coronado had surrounded a Zuni village, demanding to speak with their leader or chief. No one came out for days, and food for the village was running low. It turned out that the Zuni were not being rebellious but just did not know what a chief was, that their society had no hierarchy of rulers such as Europeans had. The village was led by a group of older men who acted as a council, a definite resemblance to Lemurian leadership at its best.

Additional observations disclosed further examples of Lemurian ways of thinking and lifestyle among the Zuni. Unlike many other

American Indian Tribes, Hordern commented that the Zuni were not nomads, but a sedentary group of people who centered their lives with family and community and followed fixed traditions. He noted that the Zuni had plenty to eat; yet, the land belonged to no one. That whatever they built was built to last a long time; and finally, the European principle of placing high importance or value on material things was not a philosophy understood among these Native Americans. In turn, the Zuni beliefs were rather new perceptions for the Spanish conquerors to encounter especially among a group of people they judged as "savages."

Mound Builders

As land appeared east of the Mississippi River after the pole shift, the Lemurian groups who came to settle in North America explored the new region. Edgar Cayce reading 328-1 documented that this curiosity brought the Lemurians all the way to Ohio and even western Pennsylvania: "For, the entity then set up in this new land the first of the temples from the Lemurian land, that has since been termed the Mound Builders' land. Not the present as seen, but that from which same arose."

Why would a group of people build mounds? Returning to Steiner for a moment, he mentioned in his book on *Atlantis and Lemuria* that in their homeland, Lemurians had built mounds to utilize as caves for themselves and developed great building skills to create such structures. These cave-like erections built in their homeland were first used as dwellings to provide humans with safety when the large animals were such a danger. Steiner added that the Lemurians used their imagination to create other constructions as well, but that these were not used as dwellings Turning to Montgomery, her guides wrote that when some Lemurians moved to the new lands that had recently risen in the United States, they built mounds shaped in the form of their native symbols. Although these mound-like structures were not used as dwelling places as their ancestors had done in Lemuria to escape the threat of large animals, these odd structures became spiritual centers for them.

In the United States, the Lemurian descendants built mounds for religious rituals. Steiner wrote that the American-born Lemurian would remodel existing hills for the sheer joy and pleasure of reshaping the earth into a recognizable symbol. In other words, building mounds was a creative endeavor Lemurians just liked to do. It should come as no surprise that the newly migrated Lemurians wanted to decorate their mounds by shaping them into familiar symbols in memory of their homeland.

These newer Lemurian mounds were also constructed with the intent to provide people with a higher place to stand to be closer to their Creator which they determined was somewhere above and beyond the sky. However, the 368-1 Cayce reading alluded to the fact that none of the Lemurian mounds are visible today. The land either eroded through time, or perhaps even trampled by unknowing humans who came to till the soil.

The second wave of Mound Builders remained a mystery to modern humans until a University of California/Davis professor published *A Land So Strange* in 2007. In his book, Dr. Andres Resandez wrote that the mounds discovered in several states that included Ohio, Kentucky, Louisiana, Alabama to name a few may be remnants of an Apalachee Chiefdom that began around 1000 A.D. Whether the people of the Apalachee culture are descendants of Lemuria or Atlantis, however, remains a mystery.

The Apalachee constructed villages from the Great Lakes down to the Gulf of Mexico, hugging the tributaries of the Mississippi River. For this reason, present-day scholars include them among the Mississippian societies claim Dr. Resandez. These natives were not primitive as they were an agricultural society who took part in long-distance networks to trade their goods. It is recorded that they were organized into a hierarchical society and left behind houses, temples, and "square-based pyramids" when their culture began to weaken because of internal disputes and wars between the villages. By the time the Europeans arrived in the 17th and 18th centuries, the Apalachee had all but disappeared, leaving only the mounds as their legacy.

Instead of sacred symbols, the Apalachee designs used for the mounds resembled pyramid-shaped ones with flat tops, a serpent or snake, horseshoe formations, conical shape, geometric forms and earthworks surrounded by moats or aligned with the stars such as Orion's belt. At this time, only the ancient builders themselves could explain why they selected the shapes they did to design their mounds.

Mexico

As Mexico was within easy access from Lemuria by ship, the Lemurians established several colonies on its coastline. The original settlements were destroyed when the mountains emerged during climate changes, but the undaunted Lemurians just rebuilt their homes at the higher altitudes. One colony the Lemurians constructed just a few miles northwest of the present site of Mexico City gained much attention in modern times when William Niven made archeological discoveries there in the early 20th century.

Niven, a mineralogist, began an archaeological dig 29 miles north of Mexico City in the 1920's, resulting in the discovery of three prehistoric cities, one on top of the other, separated by deposits of boulders, gravel, and sand. Montgomery's guides explained that only ocean waves could make these kinds of deposits and now that the site is seventy-four hundred feet above sea level, there could only be one conclusion: the site once lay near sea level before mountains were formed.

Niven says he found the archeological sites when local Indians came to sell terra cotta figurines and other items to him. At first they told Niven that they found these items at the Pyramids of the Sun and Moon at San Juan Teotehuacan which was located over 25 miles away. But Niven became suspicious when the Indians returned with more objects to sell within an hour of their last visit. He offered the Indians five pesos ($2.50) if they would take him to the site where they were finding these artifacts. They agreed.

While Churchward described Niven's excavations in detail in his book *The Lost Continent of Mu*, Montgomery summarized the findings more concisely. Her guides wrote that the artifacts found at this site indicated that these ancient people were highly cultured as the frescoes and paintings on the walls predated any that were found in ancient Egypt. Statuettes were situated around a corpse at the excavated burial site and one of those forms depicted a Chinaman. This artifact raised all kinds of queries at the time as to whether or not members of the yellow race either settled in the area or were just in contact with the new Lemurian settlements in Mexico. Green jade beads were also discovered here when jade never appeared anywhere else in Mexico.

Even Edgar Cayce reading 5750-1 commented on excavations around Mexico City at this time: ". . . until the final upheaval of Atlantis, or the islands that were later upheaved, when much of the contour of the land in Central America and Mexico was changed to that similar in outline to that which may be seen in the present.

"The first temples that were erected by Iltar and his followers were destroyed at the period of change physically in the contours of the land. That now being found, and a portion already discovered that has laid in waste for many centuries, was then a combination of those peoples from Mu, Oz [Peru] and Atlantis.

"Q. Have the most important temples and pyramids been discovered?

"A. Those of the first civilization have been discovered, and have not all been opened, but their associations, their connections, are being replaced – or attempting to be rebuilt. Many of the second and third civilization may NEVER be discovered, for these would destroy the present civilization in Mexico to uncover same!"

He was right. Mexico City does sprawl on top of Niven's three ancient civilizations excavations. Additional information about the Lemurians and their descendants who once existed there may never be found, for it is not possible to move an entire city to learn about the past.

In the late 1990's, a free-lance journalist by the name of Mark Williams toured the areas of the world that were prominently associated with Lemuria for a book published in 2001 entitled *In Search of Lemuria.* He included a visit to San Miguel Amantla located approximately 25 miles from Mexico City. This town is situated in the vicinity of Niven's archaeological find almost 90 years ago.

Williams wrote that the town today was crammed with industrial factories and looked exactly what it was - a neglected, seedy suburb of Mexico City.

Rechecking his notes and making inquiries among the local people, including the police, he concluded that there was no active archeological site there, not even a museum of sorts displaying the uncovered artifacts. Apparently, Niven's discovery was abandoned with no explanations as to why. After Niven's crew left this excavated site, no one else stepped in to study or carbon-date artifacts from the three ancient cities. Strangely, it appeared as though the excavation never even happened.

Not far from this original site, Niven documented a second great find closer to the capital near Santiago Ahuizoctla. This time his excavation uncovered 2,600 tablets with glyphs etched all over them. Naturally, Niven called in his friend, James Churchward, to examine his new artifacts. Churchward claimed that the glyphs resembled those found on other ancient tablets he had examined in India, and concluded that the Mexican tablets were definitely of Lemurian origin. Niven also gave other experts the opportunity to examine his findings to verify their age and authenticity. But, where were those tablets now? Williams could not find them anywhere in Mexico.

Through a bit of detective work, the journalist finally tracked Niven's tablets to Harvard's Peabody Museum of Archeology and learned that they were carefully wrapped and kept in storage. Specialists brought in by the museum verified that the tablets were indeed made of soft volcanic rock but their final conclusions indicated that the tablets were as not as old as first believed. Williams reported that several experts agreed that the tablets were simply extremely clever frauds.

However, Niven was a respected scholar in his field and credited with several other authentic excavations in Mexico. It is doubtful that he would try to pull off a hoax like this. Moreover, it is documented that he genuinely believed the tablets to be authentic. Therefore, the questions remain to this day: who produced and buried the fake tablets, all 2,600 of them, and why?

Central America

Montgomery's guides wrote that the Maya came among the ranks of the Lemurian priestly community. The guides noted that this was a scholarly group who had developed a sophisticated process of recording time in relation to the stars and planets. Their work had already taken hundreds of thousands of years, and they brought all this record keeping with them as they migrated to a new location to continue their work. These Lemurians settled themselves in the Yucatan area and made their home here for several thousands of years before the Atlanteans arrived. However, when the immigrants from Atlantis moved into the region, these Lemurians, known today as the Maya, withdrew further north into the rain forests and jungles of Central America and into the high mountain tops to avoid contact with the newcomers.

Nevertheless, the Atlanteans continued to force themselves on the Lemurians, sometimes even kidnapping members of their community to coerce their knowledge out of them. In retaliation, the Lemurians or Maya receded further and higher into the mountains of Central America, cutting themselves off from any contact with the outside world for eons. They had no wish to fight for their rights. Many students of the Maya made the assumption that these people took to the mountains to avoid Spanish conquests. However, according to Montgomery's guides, their self-imposed exile began much earlier, during the Atlantean conquest.

The guides wrote in 1976 that the Maya were waiting for the next pole shift as that phenomena would end their record keeping responsibilities and free them from maintaining their calculations which started hundreds of thousands of years ago. In attempting to interpret this information, it seems as though these were the Maya who shouldered the immense responsibility of keeping track of the various Mayan calendars all these millennia. If so, their long count calendar ended on the solstice of December 21, 2012; hopefully, these time keepers from the Lemurian age are now free of their enormous responsibilities.

South America

Since Lemurians frequently traveled to Peru before their continent's final destruction, it is logical that Lemurians migrated into South America through this gateway. Montgomery's guides claimed that from Peru, Lemurians settled into Mexico and Bolivia as well. They made their homes in the northwestern portions of South America, and did not wander far from their established communities.

Eventually, the Atlanteans also explored South America and some were bold enough to travel from the Atlantic coast, where they made their first settlements, all the way to the Andes and the Pacific. It was inevitable that they would find the Lemurian communities, build their own villages near them, and over time, intermingle with them. Combining the red race (Atlantean) with the brown race (Lemurian), along with members of the black and white races who also came to South America for one reason or another, created a beautiful blend of indigenous people in South America of which the Incas were the most notable.

Although the Incas are only partly Lemurian, they maintained some of the motherland's lifestyle and customs. A Spanish conquistador by the name of Pedro de Cieza de Leon kept a diary of his time in South America, in particular Peru, from 1532 to 1550 when he returned to Spain. He expressed admiration for the remarkable quality of the work the Incas accomplished when creating works of beauty in gold and silver, expressing his awe at how they achieved such perfection with so few tools. Leon wrote about the gold, silver, and clay specimens that were so intricately soldered together that no separation of the materials was apparent. More importantly, he mentioned his amazement that even the small boys, who hardly looked old enough to talk, knew how to make these various intricate pieces for ornamentation from pure gold, a difficult element to handle. Allowing small children to work alongside their elders and contribute to their community even at a very young age was indeed a Lemurian tradition.

The Aftermath

Approximately 38,000 years after the loss of Lemuria, Atlantis suffered its own destruction when their land disappeared beneath the Atlantic. Without the Great Crystal and Atlantean technology, travel returned to a primitive state. There were no more airships and submarine-like boats navigated by the Great Crystal to transport people from one continent to another. In fact, people could not even sail across the Atlantic Ocean for thousands of years after the sinking of Atlantis because the floating debris made it dangerous to maneuver ships through the mud only to dodge the large pieces of flotsam. The Montgomery guides affirmed that historical records described that for thousands of years the Atlantic Ocean was such a shallow and mud-covered sea that the ancient ones considered it too risky to even try to traverse it. Even Plato, the Greek philosopher, labelled the Atlantic as an impassable barrier as late as 360 B.C.

With no high tech method of transportation, many groups of people completely stopped trekking from one continent to another altogether. Lacking the ability to easily journey from place to place also brought a halt to the exchange not only of goods but also of ideas, philosophy, and learning among people. Humans became stagnant and isolated. Except for centers of learning in Egypt, India, and Peru, Montgomery's guides claimed that people became depressed, superstitious, and forgot what their purpose on earth was all about. Lacking the free-flow of materials, foods, and ideas, humans throughout the world began to deteriorate to a primitive state of being.

The strata of society known as "Things" were no longer available to be beasts of burden, so men and women now had to perform their own manual labor. When there was so much work to do just to survive, there was little time, if any, left to exercise the mind. The loss of two great civilizations indeed brought in a sad age for the survivors in the rest of the world, one comparable to the Dark Ages of Europe.

CHAPTER

9

The Lemurian Legacies and Legends

The Lemurians who made the ultimate sacrifice of leaving their homeland to establish colonies elsewhere would be sorely disappointed that most of the sacred knowledge they tried to save for future generations disappeared. However, their most important legacy, their belief of the one God or Creator, was nurtured down through the ages by some of the migrating groups and even experienced a resurgence over the last two thousand years with the spread of the Judeo-Christian and Islamic faiths.

Because Lemuria disappeared so long ago, no one expects anything of the lost civilization to still exist today. However, unknown to most people, the Lemurians have subsequently left a few large and some small legacies behind.

Land Legacy

Not all of the Lemurian continent slipped under the Pacific that fateful night 50,000 years ago. The ancient civilization left us with a legacy of land areas in addition to their mountaintops that make up Hawaii, Tahiti, and other Polynesian Islands today. The Edgar Cayce readings, Cerve, and Montgomery's guides all report that California including the Sierra Nevada mountain range and the Baja Peninsula once existed as a portion of the lost continent.

". . . when there became an activity in which those portions of the land were discovered from what was left of Lemuria, or Mu – in what is now lower California, portions of the valleys of death, the entity journeyed there to see, to know[,]" said Edgar Cayce reading

1473-1. The "valley of death" is of course Death Valley where several rock formations contained strange and undecipherable symbols which Churchward had already claimed to be of Lemurian origin.

How this phenomena happened, no one knows. Plausible explanations include either this eastern section of Lemuria was on a different plate than the rest of the continent, or this portion of land severed itself from the rest of Lemuria to remain above water and became an island. Eventually, through continental drift, the island remnant linked itself with the North American plate. Today, it is taken for granted that California and the Baja Peninsula were always a part of North America. Apparently, and to the surprise of many, this is not the case.

People have wondered for years why the two mountain ranges of the Rocky Mountains and the Sierra Nevada existed side by side. The explanation is now a simple one. The Rockies originally belonged to the continent of North America, while the Sierra Nevada were mountain ranges in Lemuria. When the Lemurian land remnant attached itself to the North American continent, the world now had two separate and independent mountain ranges from two different continents located next to each other.

In yet another Edgar Cayce reading, 509-1, someone was told that in a past life, he had established a temple of worship for the people who had left Lemuria, escaping from the continent that was sliding into the sea. "The entity, in the name Oeueou, established near what is now Santa Barbara the temple to the sun and moon . . ." Although this temple is long gone, the reading reinforces the fact that California, whether an island or part of North America at this time, became populated by Lemurians as they established a new home for their descendants.

Cerve tried to logically provide proof that California and the Baja peninsula were once island remnants of Lemuria. First, he pointed to the Nancy Globe found in the 16th century and now on display in the town hall of Nancy, France. He claimed that this globe, whose creation date is unknown, shows California as an island off the coast of the North American continent. The globe does indeed show several small islands off the North American coastline, but none resembled the size and shape of California and the Baja. However, to Cerve's credit, the western portion of North America was pictured on the Nancy Globe without the Baja peninsula.

Secondly, Cerve pointed to the word "California" and claimed that the state was named after Queen Califa, a queen from a legendary Spanish story, a popular one told and re-told prior to the Crusades. Apparently, Queen Califa ruled an island which was named after her; and that legendary island of California was described as a paradise. Cerve stated that while the characters in the story sounded mystical and starry-eyed, it was apparent that the tale had enough factual information on the natural environment that led him to believe someone had actually seen this island sometime before recorded history and before California became a part of North America.

Another supportive reason Cerve gave for why California did not originally belong to North America involved the character of the people residing on the West coast. He drew attention to their low-key attitude accompanied by a determination to make pleasure a priority in life with no adverse effects on business. Californians knew how to balance both amusement and work in their lives. In contrast, Cerve pointed out that people living in the east believed that in order to be successful, their time and focus had to be emphatically placed on money and business only. In essence, he attempted to prove that the vibrations in the east, carrying mark residue from the intense and frenzied Atlantean lifestyle influence, contrasted sharply with the vibrations in California where the peaceful and joyful energy of the Lemurians was still reflected in the people living there today.

Cerve also claimed that California's plant life differed from any to be found in the rest of the United States which he believed supported the fact that the state did not originate as part of the North American continent. He points to lemon and avocado trees, for instance, which once grew only in California. Also the fascinating, giant Sequoia trees, hundreds of years old, were not found anywhere else in the world either.

Finally, Cerve presented the fact that ferns and palms among other plants that need special care and attention to survive in the east grew effortlessly and without nurturing of any kind on the west coast.

One must admit that if there had been no other paranormal source to substantiate his claim, Cerve did an admirable job with his arguments to persuade that California presented a uniqueness that could not be compared to any other area the North American continent had to offer.

Another rather large additional land mass that once belonged to Lemuria remains today attached to the South American continent. To the amazement of many, the Cayce readings (362-13), and only the readings, provided the startling information that the mountain range known as the Andes Mountains remained above water after the pole shift. These mountains, on the eastern shores of Lemuria, also escaped the fate of the rest of the continent, and again, probably through continental drift, eventually attached themselves to the South American continent at some time in the past, looking as though they always belonged there. Today, they are considered among the highest and longest mountain ranges in the world. Although the peaceful and harmonious vibrations of Lemuria have diminished, some of their beautiful energy does still remain in the Andes, with the land that was left behind.

Columns Legacy

During the Golden Age of Lemuria, the people indicated the location and even the entrance of their temples through wooden poles. Over the years, the wooden poles were transformed and other types of materials such as marble, and larger pillars or columns were developed, although the round shape of the original wooden poles was kept.

The use of columns to indicate sacred space is one the Lemurian descendants took with them to other lands and shared this legacy with other people throughout the world. The Maoris of New Zealand, direct descendants of the Lemurians, placed columns at the entrance of their villages to indicate that they considered their entire villages as sacred space. Eventually, designs such as pictures or hieroglyphics and sacred symbols were etched onto the columns to remind people of the sacredness of the space they were about to enter.

Columns became a part of the architecture when designing temples or places of worship throughout the ancient world. Examine the ruins of temples in India along with Egyptian temple architecture, and columns will be found marking sacred space. The Greeks are among the first people who broke with tradition and designed their secular buildings with columns, disregarding their intended symbolic use. The purpose of the columns as an indication of sacred space finally lost its original meaning either because people deliberately decided to ignore their significance or had forgotten their original intent. Even today, people consider columns as a part of an architectural structure and attach no further meaning to them other than elegance.

In the Pacific Northwest, the Lemurian legacy of the column was transformed in a very different and interesting way. According to Edgar Cayce reading 630-2, the Lemurian descendants here modified the columns by carving them into totem poles. Their designs for the totem poles varied from depicting a family's lineage to illustrating a historic or important event. Traditionally, the highest figures on the totem pole indicated the most important image and if the totem pole indicated family lineage, the latest addition was carved on top. However, among some indigenous families, the latest family addition or the most important part of an event was etched on the bottom of the pole instead of the top. It is apparent that there were no definitive rules in the carving of a totem pole. It was fashioned and etched at the discretion of the artist.

Early missionaries in the northwest thought the natives worshipped their totem poles. Nothing could be further from the truth, as these poles usually went up and remained until they deteriorated, which they did eventually since they were made of wood. No attempt at restoration was ever made and the faded totems were simply taken down and destroyed. However, the belief that the totem poles were items of worship led to a ban against them until the mid-twentieth century when a new respect for native art permeated the modern art world and brought a revival of these structures.

Toning Legacy

Toning is expressing and sustaining the sound of a vowel out-loud until its vibration can be felt in other parts of the body. According to Thyme and Montgomery's guides, the ancient Lemurians used certain sounds for toning which vibrated the body and elevated the spiritual centers or chakras. God or the Creator was considered by the ancient people as so magnificent that His name was seldom used aloud. When it came to writing, the Lemurians created a symbol of a sun with moon at crescent as a symbol to represent their Deity. When necessary to speak the Creator's name, the symbol was translated to "O" for the sun and "hum" for the crescent which became the sound of OM where the mouth opens to pronounce the O and closed to pronounce the hum.

The mystical incantation of "Om" is still used by many meditators today. This and other ancient toning sounds are also present in Gregorian chants and often used as mantras. Thyme explains that the Buddhist monks still remember how to vocally merge two tones into one to create what they believe to be an extremely holy sound. The vibrations emanating with this sound benefits not only the person producing it but also moves everyone within hearing distance as well.

Ley Lines Legacy

The Lemurian civilization identified ley lines on their continent and made a special effort to build their communities on them. These ley lines, considered to be the nerve pathways of the earth, are also known today as "grids." Besides these grids, the Lemurians were also sensitive to the earth's vortexes, an area of the earth with enormous amounts of energy swirling and spinning in a spiral shape while remaining in place underground. According to Thyme, the Lemurians called these vortexes, energy stations. Vortexes affect different people in different ways, but they all acutely enhance spiritual and psychic abilities. To take full advantage of these energy vortexes, or energy stations, the Lemurians built their Golden Temples on top of them.

The Lemurian knowledge of ley lines or grids and vortexes

remained in the world for several millennia after the motherland disappeared. Many sacred sites people visit today were built where they are because of ancient people's experience in honoring the earth's natural energy lines. Tom Dongo, author of *The Mysteries of Sedona*, states that the Pyramids of Egypt and those of Mexico, as well as such other ancient sites as Stonehenge and Avebury to name a few, were all built to deliberately take full advantage of the energy the earth generates through its grids or ley lines.

Although thousands of miles apart, many sacred sites are situated on the same ley line and are, therefore, energetically connected to each other much the same way the Lemurian communities were connected if they were built on the same grid lines. For instance, Glastonbury, England, Mt. Shasta, CA, and Lake Taupo, New Zealand are all connected because they were built on the same ley line reports Dongo. Other sites that are verified as connected using 21st century technical instruments include Angkor Watt in Cambodia with Machu Picchu in Peru; Kathmandu in Nepal with Easter Island in the South Pacific Ocean; and Sedona, Arizona with Amsterdam in the Netherlands and with the St. Paul Islands in the Indian Ocean. And these are only a few connections as there are many more.

Unfortunately, this knowledge of the earth's energy field was lost for hundreds if not thousands of years. However, this sacred knowledge was recently rediscovered. In 1921, Englishman Alfred Watkins noticed that footpaths, traveled by people since ancient times, ran straight for miles and miles over the countryside. Upon further study, he realized that England had hundreds of these old footpaths that traversed each other. Calling them "leys" or "leas", he determined that they were paths the ancient people of Britain used as trade routes.

The study of ley lines continued in the mid 1960's when John Michell, an English writer, wrote extensively about Atlantis and other strange phenomena. He noted that many UFO sightings happened near ley lines, and realized that ley lines could be more easily seen from the air. Michell also learned that even the Chinese knew about the occurrence of ley lines but called them *lung mei*, or dragon paths. He discovered that ley lines go through several types of sacred sites which include burial mounds, old churches, and ancient monuments like Stonehenge. Michell's writings on the subject of ley lines has caught the attention of the modern world and a small part of the ancient Lemurian sacred knowledge of the earth's energy is gaining notice once more.

The Conch Legacy

In ancient Lemuria, the people used conch shells to announce a call to meetings, the birth of a child, and a beginning of an important community event such as a ritual or celebration. Although the conch as the "call" instrument for special occasions is not used anymore, the tradition of announcing the start of a happening in some way is the Lemurian legacy that has survived.

When Lytle Robinson wrote *Edgar Cayce's Origin and Destiny of Man,* he mentioned the lengthy and extravagant celebration planned to finish The Great Pyramid of Giza with a capstone. The event was announced to the people by a loud clanking of metal. Although the ceremony took place somewhere between 9,000 and 10,000 B.C., this method of announcing an event, a Lemurian tradition, was still remembered thousands of years after the disappearance of the continent. The "call" that prefaces a special event did not originate in Egypt, however, but in Lemuria. As some Lemurians did make their home in Egypt after the pole shift, it might be their influence which continued their traditions at that important historical event – finishing the Great Pyramid of Giza.

Lytle then points to other instances when an instrument of some sort is utilized to summon people to celebrate an occasion such as ringing the church bells as an invitation to prayer or worship or to usher in a New Year. With a little reflection, everyone can remember occasions and events when a "call" at the start of something special is still prevalent in the modern world, even to the playing or singing of "The Star-Spangle Banner" before every sports event. It is just that no one remembers that the tradition began tens of thousands of years ago in Lemuria with a conch shell.

Legends

Although the information that follows are considered "legends," there are people who believe that these narratives are true. The stories on the strange phenomena surrounding the environs of Mt. Shasta, come from Wishar Cerve's book on *Lemuria.* He is the only source for these mysterious reports documented by the local people of Mt. Shasta until the mid-1930s. *Telos* is a series of three books written by channeler Aurelia Louise Jones who reports that there are Lemurians living under Mt. Shasta, waiting for the time to emerge above ground to help humankind adjust to the changes to come. As with Cerve, these books are the only source for this information.

Mt. Shasta

Located at the extreme north end of the Sierra Nevada, Mt. Shasta is situated in Northern California about 45 miles from the Oregon border and not far from the Klamath Lake area. It is believed that it is currently the home of Lemurians who escaped the destruction of their continent thousands of years ago and are hiding high up in the mountain, avoiding contact with the modern world at all cost. People from different walks of life, from scientists, residents, to tourists, have reported strange and mysterious occurrences around Mt. Shasta.

Occasional sightings of people emerging from a forested area at the foot of the mountain have been reported, but as soon as these strangers realized they were seen, they immediately melted into the trees and disappeared completely. Their departure is so abrupt that no one who spotted them had time to snap a picture. Even cattle, a species never seen in America before, and sometimes seen meandering along the side of highways leading to Mt. Shasta play the same disappearing act whenever a modern human on foot or in a car came within their line of sight.

Cerve wrote that sporadically, strangers, dressed in a fashion unfamiliar to the locals and totally different from any mode of dress seen on a California indigenous person, would appear in small near-by towns to exchange a bit of gold for products. They kept to themselves as much as possible, and never answered any questions about who they were and where they came from. Cerve was told that whenever they spoke, they had a slight British accent. These strangers also never took any change from the gold transaction which was usually of far greater value than the items purchased, giving the impression that they had no interest or need for money.

Infrequently, reports of a large fire burning in the woods circulated among the locals. Cerve wrote that the fire didn't appear to be fueled by wood, oil or gasoline. However, it emanated a very brilliant, white light that bordered on a violet-blue hue. Whenever there was a ceremony using these large fires, the celebrations were performed three times in the space of twenty-four hours, namely, at sunrise, sunset, and midnight of the same day.

Apparently, at the midnight ceremony, beams of bright light of an unknown origin were cast high up into the trees. If these beams of light were aimed in the direction of the mountain, buildings could be seen. There were reports of gold-plated domes and buildings built of marble and onyx. Moreover, if the wind blew in the right direction, people residing in nearby towns could even hear strange chanting and peculiar, yet beautiful music.

Of course, investigators came to explore these peculiar sightings and reports, but they were never able to travel very far up the mountain. The residents of Mt. Shasta protected themselves in one of two ways, apparently. First, investigators could encounter concealed persons of a very large size who would lift them up, turn them from their destination of the interior of Mt. Shasta, and forcibly impressed upon them to walk away from the mountain as quickly as possible. Another method used was to surround investigators with unusual and strange vibrations or some kind of invisible energy that would enable them to move in one direction only, namely, away from their original destination.

If attempts to explore Mt. Shasta were done by car, investigators found that the car would only go so far before it stopped functioning properly. The electric circuit would fail and not until passengers emerged from the car to push it around and aim it back down the mountain did the malfunction suddenly disappear and the car operated properly once more.

Needless to say, the mysterious residents of Mt. Shasta are still an unexplained phenomena and retain their privacy to this day – if they really do exist.

Telos

Telos is an underground city built under Mt. Shasta before Lemuria was completely destroyed, claimed Aurelia Louis Jones, a channeler for the Lemurian High Priest, Adama. She wrote that the 20 mile long, 5-level city was tunneled under the mountain with the intent of preserving Lemurian records. Apparently, Telos was created to accommodate over 200,000 Lemurians but only 25,000 managed to gain the shelter before their homeland disappeared altogether. Adama explained that the destruction occurred earlier than anticipated and many people became trapped, unable to leave. According to Jones, Telos is the underground home to 1,500,000 people at the present time.

Full spectrum light floods the city of Telos on all 5-levels, providing all the light humans, animals, and plants require for survival. No one needs to leave the safety of the city to go outside the mountain to gain sunlight. What is necessary for existence is provided. Food is grown hydroponically, using very little soil and much water, both free of any chemicals although minerals are added to the water. Adama reports that crops are produced on a constant basis and plants grow rather quickly. Everyone is vegetarian and no animals are killed to provide food for human consumption. Even the animals are vegetarians, and species are not pitted against each other to be killed and eaten.

Jones writes that their system of government consists of two levels. There is a king by the name of Ra and a queen, Rana Mu. Next in line is the Lemurian Council which is comprised of 12 people, six men and six women, to provide a balance between male and female points of view. The High Priest, Adama, serves as the thirteenth member of the council and makes final decisions when there is a tie vote among the council members.

Besides accomplishing self-sufficiency while being totally underground, the people of Telos claim they also discovered how to maintain immortality. Jones' three book narrative describes life in

Telos as perfect and makes the underground city sound comparable to nirvana or a Shangri-la.

Both the underground city of Telos and the mysterious incidents surrounding Mt. Shasta sound magical, intriguing, and almost romantic. Whether this information is true and these Lemurians really do exist is difficult to discern. It will be up to each individual to decide whether or not to believe these legends.

CHAPTER

10

THE LEMURIAN RETURN

Ruth Montgomery's guides reported that the Lemurians reincarnated in cycles. In fact, an influx of Lemurian souls on earth occurred only when humanity appeared ready to accept a new paradigm shift. Examples of these shifts include the European Renaissance of the 14th and 15th centuries and the American fight for independence in the 18th century. That means that re-embodied Lemurians were present for the creation of the Declaration of Independence and the Constitution as both documents represented critical shifts in thinking for humanity. Montgomery's guides also mentioned that Thomas Jefferson, Benjamin Franklin, and George Washington experienced both Lemurian and Atlantean lifetimes, and as products of both civilizations, were interested in inventions because of their Atlantean legacy, and yet, exhibited an idealistic and democratic philosophy because of their Lemurian inheritance.

Montgomery's guides added that the Lemurians were not currently in physical form at the time her book was published (1970's) as humanity had become obsessed with new technical inventions and material acquisitions. The lack of Lemurian influence explains the void of any new thought and philosophical ideas in the modern world. Actually, the strides made in technology during the late 20th and early 21st centuries indicate that reincarnated Atlanteans with their love of new inventions and their penchant for aggressive competition are the prevalent influences at this time in human history. However, this Atlantean mindset is about to change.

Lemurian Influence

Although the Lemurians may not have been physically present during the late 20th century, they managed to infuse some of the earth's people with their gentle energy as well as their love and respect for nature. Their success is visible in the environmental issues that have emerged to the forefront, generating awareness and interest in the debilitating health of the planet. Groups launched campaigns to educate the general public on the damage done to the ecosystem with unconscious littering and waste dumping in the oceans; the dangers of accepting genetically modified (GMO) food; and the urgency of supporting local farmers with their use of organic gardening methods instead of purchasing mass produced food raised with heavy doses of pesticides.

It is Lemurian influence that also aided in creating public intolerance of animal abuse as well as increasing awareness of the impending extinction of several animal species; for example, polar bears because of climate change and elephants because of the unnecessary mass murders of their herds by humans just to extract the tusks. Dr. Kathy Callahan in her book, *Our Origin and Destiny*, emphasized how contingencies to end these atrocities are now in place in the modern world as groups of people take the lead to repair the ecological damage done to the earth while others educate the rest of the population about the results to humanity if the abuse to nature continues. Callahan admonishes that destruction to the planet and nature for the purposes of greed, modern conveniences, and technology must never happen again.

In spite of the positive implementations made on environmental issues, however, the present human condition is experiencing problems on several other fronts. Nature is currently taking a toll on humankind in all parts of the world in the form of debilitating storms, volcanic eruptions, violent hurricanes, tornadoes, and tsunamis. All of these are a part of the earth changes predicted for this timeframe, resulting in climate changes which in turn affect crops, disrupt food distribution, and eventually raise the food prices to unprecedented levels. On the financial front, because of globalization, mounting debts and economic setbacks in one nation affect other countries all over the world. The upcoming scarcity and rising prices of oil has already taken a toll on the cost of transportation and travel.

Humankind has dealt with all of these problems before, but as Gregg Braden points out in his book, *The Turning Point*, humans have not had to face all these crises at the same time. Moreover, he indicates that none of these can currently be solved with 20th century solutions because the world as humans have known it over the last several decades is simply gone and will not return.

Braden blends predictions from indigenous peoples with current scientific data to show that the world is not quite on the brink of extinction, however. As people awaken to the fact that some kind of shift is already happening and that life will not return to "normal" or the way "it used to be," they will find 21st century ways to solve the difficulties facing them. Braden also warns though that before people find and implement these necessary solutions, something else has to happen first: a shift in thinking.

His words echo a prophecy that has come down through the ages from many sources, including the post-2012 prophecies from the Mayans, that humankind will experience a consciousness shift, although no one knows exactly what that is or when it will happen.

Until the turn of this century, the phrase "consciousness shift" embodied only words bantered around, lifting many an eyebrow in consternation or disbelief but with no real understanding of what the concept really meant or what humans can expect to see or feel. However, author, lecturer, and teacher, Drunvalo Melchisedek, provides people with more details about this coming wonder with the 2007 publication of his book, *Serpent of Light: Beyond 2012*, followed several years later with his DVD production entitled, *The Birth of a New Humanity*.

Drunvalo's explanations defy the mind's logic but not the wisdom of the heart. A student at Berkeley with a major in fine arts and a minor in physics and mathematics, he walked away from the modern world to follow his heart and inner guidance. In 1971, he began the study of sacred geometry and learned about earth's energies from indigenous people who have kept the planet's mysteries to themselves. Drunvalo also studied with well over ninety spiritual teachers from all over the world. He considers himself to be a white man in an indigenous body, and following native ways, lives from the heart and not the mind.

The reason Drunvalo's work is important to the topic of Lemuria is that his experiences with energy work concerning the earth occurred in and around ancient Lemurian land. It is almost as though a reactivation of former Lemurian energy of love, harmony and the knowledge of Oneness is underway. If so, the shifts, including a consciousness shift or a shift in thinking, will change the human evolutionary path away from its present state of chaos and problems towards a path of the higher consciousness beliefs of love, harmony, peace, and Oneness, the ancient Lemurian beliefs.

Earth's Energy Shift

Since the earth is a living organism, Drunvalo explains that it contains a snake-like energy, one that resembles and moves much like a serpent. It is technically called a kundalini energy and it resides inside the earth. One end is anchored to the core of the earth while the other is free to travel anywhere in the world, thrusting itself back and forth much as a serpent would move. For this reason, it is known among people familiar with the earth's energy as the Serpent of Light.

The Serpent of Light is a spiritual energy that coils itself down inside the earth and hibernates there for 13,000 years at a time. Wherever it settles, Drunvalo points out that it motivates the people of that region to become enlightened and encourages them to become spiritual teachers to the rest of the world. After 13,000 years in one location, the Serpent of Light then moves to a new home. Until recently, the Earth's Kundalini home was in Tibet where the Great White Pyramid was built to indicate its exact position. Infusing spiritual energy within a wide area around Tibet, some great souls emerged from this vicinity, leaving an indelible mark on the history of humankind. Serving as examples of the more prominent spiritual contributions include Lao Tzu, author of Tao Te Ching; the Buddha, the founder of a great religious center; and the invention of the I-Ching.

In 1949, China invaded Tibet. In 1959, China violently suppressed a Tibetan uprising that resulted in the Dalai Lama leaving the area to reside in India. Drunvalo explains that the Serpent of Light left Tibet with him. Although it seemed as though the Dalai Lama had summoned it to follow him, the reality was that the Age of Aquarius was dawning, and according to the Mayan calendar, it was time for the Earth's Kundalini energy or Serpent of Light to find a new home. Therefore, it did not remain in India with the Dalai Lama, but continued its movement and traveled the world.

In the late 1960's, Drunvalo documented that the Earth's Kundalini energy journeyed down the North American continent, through Canada, into the United States, into Mexico, Belize, Guatemala, and through Central America. Upon reaching Panama, its path was blocked; it could not continue. The construction of the Panama Canal had not only physically separated the two continents of North and South America, but it had also severed the energy of the ley lines between the continents as well. This energy split prevented the Earth's Kundalini energy from going any further and it was literally blocked from getting across into South America. According to Drunvalo, the event came as a complete surprise to the indigenous tribes, except for the Mayans.

Drunvalo explains that the Maya consulted their calendar and when the time was right, performed a special ceremony called the Ceremony of the Eagle and the Condor. With the Eagle as the representation of North America, and the Condor as the representation of South America, Drunvalo claimed that this ceremony, enacted with a multitude of indigenous people present, helped the Serpent of Light move across the Panama Canal to its final destination in South America.

In 2001, tribes from all over the Americas, numbering more than 500 of them by Drunvalo's estimate, began the work of moving the Serpent of Light across the Panama Canal. It took three days of meditation before the first trickle of energy finally entered Columbia and eventually moved into every area, every region of South America. At the same time, Drunvalo wrote, 112 tribes sat in a circle high up in the Andes, waiting to welcome the Serpent of Light when it would arrive in the exact location the Maya had predicted.

According to Drunvalo, the Serpent of Light is indeed nestled in its designated spot in the Andes Mountains of Chile, on the western side of the mountain range near Peru. It is safely resting in its new home for the next 13,000 years, in mountains that were once a part of Lemuria, and overlooking the area where the lost continent once existed although not too many people know that. Phase one of the expected energy shifts was completed and it is interesting to note that the Serpent of Light settled itself in the midst of ancient Lemurian energy.

Male and Female Energy Shifts

A second energy shift occurred shortly before the turn of the 21st century which few people know about. This one took place on the island of Kauai and Drunvalo's presence allowed him to write an account of this energy transfer. Although he describes the events of that energy shift in detail, the most important thing to know is that it involves a ceremony that happens every 12,920 years, shifting the energy between male and female. At this time in human history, the power exchange went from the male to the female. The result of this ceremony will see a resurgence of female energy that will become a dominant influence on humanity for the next 12,920 years.

Drunvalo explains that females at the present time are very much pulled into the masculine world as women are encouraged to think too much like men in order to step into positions of power. With the change of energy, females can step back into their more creative and intuitive ways of thinking to guide the world back into the light. Drunvalo claims that they will also now be ready for the changes to come. The dominance of female energy in the world would not have been possible if the present imbalance between male and female energy had been maintained.

It cannot be just a coincidence to have the transference of power of male to female energy happen on land that was once a part of the Lemurian continent and home to a civilization that was based on a matriarchal society. Once more it seems as though a reactivation of ancient Lemurian energy is at work here bringing a plentiful, strong female energy and presence in the world once again.

These predictions seem difficult to believe as one examines the present time, but Drunvalo wrote that the world would begin to see the shift to the female energy near the years 2012 – 2013. If one does examine the current status of women in modern western society, there are vast improvements made to place women in positions of power. In 2008, Harvard University named Drew Gilpin Faust as the first female president of a university formally known as a male center of power. Shortly thereafter, Brown University in Rhode Island also selected a female to be their president. Large western corporations such as Kraft Foods, Pepsico, and Facebook have recently seen females capture the top leadership roles. Women are also becoming the head of nations and the world observed a women becoming the president of Brazil and another the Chancellor of Germany. The list of females moving into positions of power expands with every passing year.

Although there are still sections in the world that are trying to keep females and the female energy down through male domination, these hold-outs will not continue for long. Moreover, it is important to note that the stronger female energy is not here to dominate but rather to partner with the male energies and to temper the male aptitude to solve differences through war as well as purge the present human tendency for competition and aggression.

The Consciousness Energy Grid

Drunvalo reported that he made several trips to the Andes after the Serpent of Light settled there only to feel no energy emanating from it at all. Apparently, the Earth's Kundalini could or would not function without the consciousness grid energy operating as well. The consciousness grid is an invisible electromagnetic energy shield surrounding the earth. Under construction for 13,000 years, it was spiritually built using the science of geomancy and completed in 2008 says Drunvalo. The purpose of this grid is to help generate the long predicted human shift in consciousness or thinking.

Although the Earth's Kundalini energy was in place, the consciousness grid could not operate because, as Drunvalo explained, the geometry of the unseen grid surrounding the planet was off. Apparently, in some parts of the world, people had done things near certain sacred sites and those actions or events needed to be forgiven. According to Drunvalo, these sacred sites were of utmost importance as they provided the energy on the ground to build and connect with the invisible consciousness grid above the earth. Performing a sacred ceremony for forgiveness at the sacred site suffering from the disturbance eradicated the counterbalance in the grid above it.

After one of these forgiveness ceremonies on Easter Island, Drunvalo reported that a golden light came down from the sky and kept swirling around the people participating in the ceremony for at least ten minutes. Photos taken of the golden light confirmed his description and the phenomena parallels the same descriptive golden light that bathed the Lemurian Sacred Temples in ancient times according to Thyme. Drunvalo said that the golden light that enveloped him and his fellow participants felt like God just as the Lemurians also expressed that the Golden Light beaming into their Temples felt like their Creator or God. The comparative descriptions from Thyme and Drunvalo are astounding.

The Consciousness Energy grid was launched on the island of Moorea in the Pacific in 2008 when it was finally able to work in tandem with the Serpent of Light. Again, it is interesting to note that the launch of the grid happened on ancient Lemurian land, on a heart-shaped island in the Pacific that contains strong female energy. The energy combination from the Serpent of Light and the consciousness grid will serve humanity by bringing about the consciousness shift, which according to the Mayans, will happen instantaneously, and according to Drunvalo, to start anytime between 2008 and 2015. The theory of the 100th monkey syndrome is probably at work here. When a certain number of humans are awakened or prioritize spirituality in their lives, the consciousness shift will happen.

Drunvalo actually calls this shift the Ascension – a lifting of human consciousness and thinking to higher spiritual levels. The consciousness shift will have humans thinking more about their relationship to the world and the oneness of all beings rather than just thinking about themselves. They will make decisions that will not "take" things from the environment but work in harmony with nature and the world's natural ecosystem. That is indeed a resurgence of the ancient Lemurian higher consciousness energy exhibited through their way of living. This ancient Lemurian energy is now returning to earth for the first time since the civilization's demise.

Consciousness Shift and Scientific Research

Actually, the scientific community is also intimating that there are shifts in thinking on the horizon. Whereas humans have thought for hundreds of years that everyone and everything is separate, current research is bringing to light that everything in the world is actually interconnected. In addition, where humans believed for centuries that competition is a necessary way of life, recent studies find that cooperation is highly preferable to rivalry and war.

Braden explains that the shift will see humans making a choice between cooperation and competition in the future. In citing the work of Alfie Kohn, author of *No Contest* published in 1992, Braden reports that Kohn reviewed over four hundred studies done on cooperation versus competition. His research conclusively established that competition is destructive and that cooperation is highly beneficial in every section of life.

Humankind's current way of thinking began with the acceptance of the scientific method approximately three hundred years ago, claims Braden. The premise of any scientific study began with the assumption that everyone and everything is separate. Moreover, another reason for the world's belief in separation was Darwin's theory of the survival of the fittest, writes Marc Ian Barasch, author of *Field Notes on the Compassionate Life*. In actuality, continues Barasch, Darwin mentioned the word "survival" only twice in his book, *The Descent of Man*, and the word "love" 95 times. Furthermore, more proof is now accumulating through studies and experiments that conclusively points to the fact that nature does not live competitively, but actually operates very democratically and quite cooperatively.

Braden writes that competition permeates modern humanity's worldview so deeply that people are totally unaware what a tremendous influence it exerts on every aspect of life. It is the belief in competition that has led humanity to think that people are separate from one another and indeed very separate from the natural world. Yet, Braden concludes, humans were created with nature, existed as a part of the natural world since the beginning even when unaware of the connection, and the human tie to nature will never end. In other words, humans and nature are all one and people need to start living and making decisions with that ancient Lemurian concept in mind.

As if to solidify that this is the future direction for humanity, Hollywood director, Tom Shadyak, who directed such blockbuster movies as *Ace Ventura* and *Bruce Almighty* to name a few, verifies that humans will begin to cooperate with each other in his 2012 documentary, *I AM*. Interviewing leading authors and other experts on the subject of "what's wrong with the world," Shadyak discussed with investigative journalist, Lynne McTaggart, how humans and nature are actually energetically interconnected and part of a greater whole. McTaggart's recent publication of her book, *The Field: The Quest for the Secret Force of the Universe*, contains documentation from reliable sources of how interrelated the entire universe is.

Thom Hartmann, psychoanalyst, radio commentator, and author of *The Last Hours of Ancient Sunlight*, reiterated the same information with the additional data that cooperation is actually a part of the human DNA. Humans are built for cooperation and connected with all life at some deep level, contends Hartmann. Moreover, he shares the notion that humans are also wired for a sense of community, not separateness, which is the lonely road people have followed for the past several hundred years.

Prophecy Supports Science

Although the soul journey in the Fourth Root Race or Adamic bodies is not over by any means, Edgar Cayce reading 5748-6 did predict that a Fifth Root Race was coming. This leads to the expectation that humanity will probably experience some changes to the physical body sometime in the future. Unfortunately, the reading added no additional information as to what could be expected. However, during one of Carol Chapman's regressions dealing with the Root Races (see Chapter 2), she was given a small preview of things to come. She reported seeing that the Fifth Root Race will use telepathy again for communication, will not experience the aging process, and will be kind and loving because of the fulfillment they will feel within themselves.

Fear will not exist in their psyche as this negative emotion will be replaced with love, explained Chapman. "The Fifth Root Race won't have rebellion. They'll live love . . . They won't make war because they are peaceful. When they are challenged, their first thought won't be to fight. They'll have different reactions than we do. They won't destroy nature like we do because they won't be afraid. They will know how to cooperate with nature . . . but they won't wallow in the physical or create fantastic things that say how great they are. Their first purpose will be to help each other."

Chapman's descriptions illustrate the changes in consciousness the Fifth Root Race will experience in addition to possible changes to the physical body. What is more astonishing, however, is to realize her details support what life could become once humanity's shift in consciousness transpires. Chapman's information, obtained through regression, not only serves to add one more substantiation of the changes expected through that shift in consciousness, but her experience also confirms that the coming shift will return humanity to the ideal spiritual and mental existence the ancient Lemurians once enjoyed.

The Return to Lemurian Values

The stage is set and all is ready for a new evolutionary path humanity is to follow. The Earth's Kundalini energy is settled in South America, the power and energy shift from male to female is completed, and the consciousness grid is connected to the Serpent of Light, poised to help mankind with this paradigm shift. That new consciousness is gaining more definition, and even the scientific world is recognizing its existence as they realize that nature does not live in "separateness" and neither should humanity. As more and more humans learn that they are, as Hartman says, "hard-wired" for cooperation and a sense of living in community, competition and all its destructiveness will be left behind.

The Lemurians used the channeler, Lauren Thyme, to let humankind know that the most spiritual of all civilizations considered themselves failures. In their eyes, they failed at not embracing living fully in the physical body. They claimed they were afraid to become too much of the earth, learning too late that this task was exactly what they were supposed to do. They were to remain in their higher consciousness while completely immersing themselves in their physical bodies. By doing so, they had the opportunity to elevate the consciousness of the entire planet so that all of humankind living on the earth could access this higher consciousness way of living.

To their credit, however, the ancient Lemurians guided the earth's people for thousands of years to the point of once again providing humanity with the opportunity to align with the higher consciousness realm the Lemurians themselves once enjoyed. This time around, humanity already resides in their physical bodies, which eliminates that first obstacle the Lemurians originally faced where they preferred to live outside their bodies rather than within them. The only step that remains is to have humanity transcend into the higher consciousness state. Humans will at long last be able to create a world that is "as above, so below."

Although some may argue that this is a utopian way of thinking, there are plenty of prophecies that foretell that the Oneness of all life is a concept that will be recognized universally once more. Jesus left the world with the inkling of what was to come when He gave humanity the famous prayer known as the Our Father. The phrase, "Thy will be done on earth as it is in Heaven," indicates that humans were meant to move towards a life lived spiritually with God or Source as their Guide and Co-creator. Moreover, even Edgar Cayce reading 294-185 predicts that the time was fast approaching for "the righteous shall inherit the earth."

In conclusion, Earth was created for beauty and happiness, and life here was never supposed to be as difficult or as unkind as humans have certainly made it. However, the story of Lemuria has come full circle and not only have the Lemurians paved the way but also revitalized their energy on earth to provide humankind the opportunity to return to the Lemurian way of life and thinking, a fulfilling existence with harmony, purpose, joy, and most importantly – love, unconditional love for everyone and everything.

ACKNOWLEDGEMENTS

Researching and writing this book in drips and drabs became a sort of hobby for me. I did this out of the sheer love of putting ideas together as well as the love of writing. I was fortunate to have so many people encourage me to keep on going while other people shared information that gave me ideas to make the story of Lemuria more alive for today's reading audience.

One of the first persons I want to thank is Joan Griffith, the daughter of Percy Tate Griffith, James Churchward's lawyer and best friend. I was discouraged at using Churchward as a source for many lovers of ancient mysteries do not consider him as a very credible resource. However, Joan provided me with a copy of her article written for *World Explorer Magazine* and I changed my mind. He may be dismissed by some experts, but the general public still associates the name of Churchward with Lemuria, or Mu as he preferred to call it. I also want to thank Joan for making me aware of her father's unpublished manuscript about his friend entitled *My Friend Churchie and His Sunken Island of Mu* which is still available in the archives of the ARE Library in Virginia Beach. It gave me not only a different view of Churchward but also a greater respect for the pioneer he was on the topic. His theories may not be proved today but no one can say with absolute certainty that he isn't right.

I can never thank my friend, author, and publisher, Carol Chapman, enough for her willingness to immediately publish my first draft of the book. Because so much of this version centered on Churchward's material, I begged her to give me time to update it. I know that if she had not been standing by to publish it, I would have given up a long time ago. Sometimes the task of combining all these sources was just too difficult and I had the tendency to put the book aside for months to take a break from the intensity. However, 10+ years is a long time to wait for a manuscript and by the time I was ready to send the book to print, Carol had moved on to other projects. I thank her for having my back all these years though, because without her support, this printed book would not be in your hands.

I also want to acknowledge Carol Hicks, a web designer and artist, who worked with Carol Chapman to design a book cover for Lemuria. The painting is a beautiful piece that could not be used at this time. However, it is my intent to develop a web site for the book and I hope Carol's painting will have a prominent position there for all to see.

I don't know why, but Scott Elliot's statement that Lemurians did not have a brain bothered me immensely. In my heart, I felt he was so wrong. In reading Steiner, I came to realize we were both right. They did not have a brain per se at the start of this civilization, but the Lemurians developed the brain over the years. As it turns out, Chapter 6 on the brain is one of my favorites and its development is thanks to Oprah Winfrey of all people. No, I never had the privilege of meeting her, but through her talk show, she brought two people to my awareness: Dr. Jill Bolte Taylor and Daniel Pink. I realized that Dr. Taylor's access only to her right brain after her stroke was exactly how the Lemurian brain worked before memory was developed. Daniel's book illustrated to me the value of the right brain in the years to come, a Lemurian return of sorts. These two authors were valuable inspirations to me for Chapter 6.

Thank you Thomas Weber for helping me with the illustrations for this chapter on the brain. These visuals made the information clearer and more understandable for the reader and I appreciate the time and effort you put into this when you had so many other projects of your own. You are a good friend.

Another person I have to thank is Shirley MacLaine for the courage to write about her insights on Lemuria in her book *The Camino*. As of today, there is no other source who describes the separation of the androgynous body into its male and female parts. The Cayce readings confirmed this really happened, but no detailed description was given.

More of Shirley's insights can be found throughout the book and I thank her for the information that gave such depth to this particular Lemurian story. She brought tears to my eyes when she stated that with the loss of the Lemurian continent, spirituality had lost its home. I felt she was so right.

I thank my little niece, Rosemarie Marcotte, fondly known as Rosie to family and friends, for drawing the three maps in Chapter 7 of this book. Well, "little niece" doesn't describe her anymore as she is now a college graduate with a marketing position in a well-known firm in New York City. However, she was only 14 at the time she drew these maps free-hand – no tracing. Rosie converted the maps to digital format for me just a few years ago. Wherever I spoke on Lemuria, one question that was asked consistently was "where was it located?" Or, "What did it look like?" I felt the inclusion of maps was very necessary to complete the book and I am so thankful for her contribution.

A big thank you also goes to a dear friend, Nancy Chrisbaum. Her encouragement was unwavering and her editing skills are second to none. Kudos needs to go to her patience as well. She was with me every step through this 20 year journey. Her most valuable contribution occurred just a few years ago when I experienced the biggest writer's block at the start of the third chapter. I could find no common thread on the description of a Lemurian. Descriptions were extreme from a reptilian body to bodies that didn't walk but floated above the ground. I was just exasperated and on the verge of dumping this whole project when Nancy simply said to write just that . . . no two sources agreed on the subject of the Lemurian appearance. That was it! The block disappeared and the rest of the book just flowed.

My biggest thank you goes to my Magnificent Five group: Toni Romano, Alice Bonnefoi, Marianna Theo, and Dr. Barbara Sikes. This group got together to read and discuss Anita Moorjani's book where she presented the idea that we should all think of ourselves as magnificent beings. The group has been together ever since. One day, someone mentioned how anxious they were to read my book on Lemuria. I was just finishing up the third chapter at the time and impulsively offered to provide them with a chapter to read every week. And that's how the book was finally written. I couldn't let this group down and pushed myself hard to finish and print 5 copies in time for each meeting. My information was so bottled-up in my head and heart that it was a relief to finally share my discoveries on Lemuria. The group provided me with critiques, corrections, and editing suggestions as well as deadlines. Without them, I might still be writing this book! So, for this reason I dedicate it to my Magnificent Ones with a very grateful thank you for being in my life.

BIBLIOGRAPHY

Allen, Eula. *Before The Beginning*. Virginia Beach, VA: A.R.E. Press, 1966.

Allen, Eula. *You Are Forever*. Virginia Beach, VA: A.R.E. Press, 1966.

Allen, Eula. *The River of Time*. Virginia Beach, VA: A.R.E. Press, 1965.

Andres, Dennis. *A Practical Guide to Sedona's Vortex Sites*. Sedona, Arizona: Meta Adventures, 2000.

Andrews, Shirley. *Lemuria and Atlantis*. Minnesota: Llewellyn Publications, 2004.

"Atlantis." *The Edgar Cayce Readings, Vo. 22*. Virginia Beach: Association for Research and Enlightenment, Inc., 1987.

Barasch, Marc Ian. *Field Notes on the Compassionate Life: In Search for the Soul of Kindness*. New York: Rodale Books, 2005.

Bauval, Robert and Gilbert, Adrian. *The Orion Mystery*. New York: Three Rivers Press, 1995.

Braden, Gregg. *The Turning Point*. California: Hay House, Inc. 2014.

Callahan, Kathy L., Ph.D. *Our Origin and Destiny*. Virginia Beach, VA: A.R.E. Press, 1996.

Cerve, Wishar. *Lemuria*. San Jose: Supreme Grand Lodge AMORC, 1997.

Chapman, Carole A. P. *The Golden Ones: From Atlantis to a New World.* Mystic, Ct: CPS, 2001.

Chapman, Carole A. P. *When We Were Gods.* Mystic, Ct: CPS, 2001.

Childress, David Hatcher. *The Lost Cities and Ancient Mysteries of South America.* Stelle, IL: Adventures Unlimited Press, 1986.

——————————. *Lost Cities of China, Central Asia and India.* Stelle, IL: Adventures Unlimited Press, 1987.

——————————. *Lost Cities of Ancient Lemuria & the Pacific.* Stelle, IL: Adventures Unlimited Press, 1988.

——————————. *Lost Cities of North and Central America.* Stelle, IL: Adventures Unlimited Press, 1992.

Churchward, Col. James. *The Lost Continent of Mu.* New York: William Edwin Rudge, 1926.

——————————. *Cosmic Forces of Mu.* New York: Ives Washburn, 1934.

——————————. *The Children of Mu.* New York: Ives Washburn, 1948.

——————————. *The Sacred Symbols of Mu.* New York: Ives Washburn, 1953.

Cori, Patricia. *Cosmos of the Soul.* Berkeley, CA : North Atlantic Books, 2008.

——————. *Atlantis Rising.* Berkeley, CA : North Atlantic Books, 2008.

Dongo, Tom. *Mysteries of Sedona.* Sedona, AZ: Hummingbird Publishing, 1988.

Earll, Tony. *Mu Revealed*. New York: Paperback Library, 1970.

Griffith, Joan T. "James Churchward and His Lost Pacific Continent: Lost Continent or Lost Cause?" Kempton, Illinois: *World Explorer Magazine*, issue & date?

Griffith, Percy Tate. *My Friend Churchie and His Sunken Island of Mu*. Unpublished manuscript 920/G 475M. Association for Research and Enlightenment Library, Virginia Beach, VA.

Hartmann, Thom. *The Last Hours of Ancient Sunlight*. New York: Broadway Books, 2004.

Hordern, Nicholas. "God, Gold and Glory." *Encyclopedia of Discovery and Exploration, Vol. 4*. London: Aldus Books Limited, 1971.

Hutton, William. *Coming Earth Changes*. Virginia Beach, VA: ARE Press, 1980.

Johnson, K. Paul. *The Masters Revealed: Madame Blavatsky and the Myth of the Great White Lodge*. Albany: State University of New York Press, 1994.

Jones, Aurelia Louise. *Revelations of the New Lemuria: Telos, Vol.1*. CA: Mount Shasta Light Publishing, 2004.

Joseph, Frank. *The Lost Civilization of Lemuria*. Rochester, Vermont: Bear & Company, 2006.

_____. *Advanced Civilization of Prehistoric America*. Rochester, Vermont: Bear & Company, 2010.

_____. *Edgar Cayce's Atlantis and Lemuria*. Virginia Beach, VA: ARE Press, 2001.

Kolbert, Elizabeth. *The Sixth Extinction: An Unnatural History*. New York: Henry Holt and Company, 2014.

Kueshana, Eklal. *The Ultimate Frontier*. Texas: The Adelphi Organization, 1992.

Landsburg, Alan. *In Search of Lost Civilizations*. New York: Bantam Books, 1976.

Little, Greg, et. al. *Ancient South America*. Memphis, TN: Eagle Wing Books, Inc., 2002.

_____. *Mound Builders*. Memphis, TN: Eagle Wing Books, Inc., 2001.

Little, Lora H., ED.D, et. al. *Secrets of the Ancient World*. Virginia Beach, VA: ARE Press, 2003.

MacLaine, Shirley. *The Camino*. New York: Pocket Books, 2000.

McTaggart, Lynne. *The Field: The Quest for the Secret Force of the Universe*. New York: Harper Perennial, 2008.

Melchizedek, Drunvalo. *Serpent of Light: Beyond 2012*. Newburyport, MA: Weiser, 2008.

Michell, John. *The View Over Atlantis*. New York: Ballantine Books, 1969.

Montgomery, Ruth. *The World to Come*. New York: Harmony Books, 1999.

_____. *The World Before*. New York: Coward, McCann, Geoghegan, 1976.

Pink, Daniel H. *A Whole New Mind: Why Right-Brainers Will Rule the Future*. New York: Riverhead Books, 2006.

Resendez, Andres. *A Land So Strange: The Epic Journey of Cabeza de Vaca*. New York: Basic Books, 2007.

Robinson, Lytle. *Edgar Cayce's Origin and Destiny of Man*. Virginia Beach, VA: A.R.E. Press, 2008.

Steiner, Rudolf. *Cosmic Memory: Atlantis and Lemuria*. New York: Rudolf Steiner Publications, 1971.

_____. *Atlantis: The Fate of a Lost Land and Its Secret Knowledge*. Sophia Books: East Sussex, England, 2001.

Scott-Elliot, William. *Legends of Atlantis and Lost Lemuria*. IL: The Theosophical Publishing House, 2000.

Sitchin, Zechariah. *The 12th Planet*. Vermont: Bear and Company, 1991.

Smolenyak, Megan Smolenyak, et. al. *Trace Your Roots with DNA*. New York: Rodale, 2004.

Subramunlyaswami, Satguru Sivaya. *The Lemurian Scrolls*. India: Himalayan Academy, 1998.

Taylor, Jill Bolte, Ph.D. *My Stroke of Insight*. New York: Viking, 2008.

Thyme, Lauren O. and Orion, Sareya. *The Lemurian Way*. Lakeville, MN: Galde Press Inc., 2001.

Waters, Frank. *Book of the Hopi*. New York: Penguin Books, 1965.

White, John, Ed. *Pole Shift*. Virginia Beach: A.R.E. Press, 2002.

Williams, Mark R. *In Search of Lemuria*. San Mateo, CA: Golden Era Books, 2001.

Wilson, Colin and Flem-Ath, Rand. *The Atlantis Blueprint*. New York: Delacorte Press, 2001.

Zapp, Ivar and Erikson, George. *Atlantis in America: Navigators of the Ancient World*. Illinois: Adventures Unlimited Press, 1998.

Media

Discover the Dreamer from Lemuria. Perf. Lazaris. 1991. Audio cassette.

The Birth of a New Humanity. Perf. Drunvalo Melchisedek. 2010. DVD.

I Am. Perf. Tom Shadyak, Thom Hartman. 2012. DVD.

Web Sites

www.lemurianconnection.com

http://en.wikipedia.org/wiki/Paleolithic

http://en.wikipedia.org/wiki/Helena_Blavatsky

http://celestialwellspring.com/lightbody.html

http://www.lemurianchoir.com/the-pineal-tones/what-is-toning

ABOUT THE AUTHOR

U NA MARCOTTE has maintained a highly successful career in a variety of fields over the years. In addition to her life-long interest in ancient civilizations, she is an avid reader, teacher, researcher and writer. Una earned a Liberal Arts degree at Marquette University and a graduate degree in Communications from the University of Wisconsin-Milwaukee. She taught high school English, Journalism, and Mass Media for nine years. She later worked for such Fortune 500 companies as the Xerox Corporation, Miller Brewing, Wang Laboratories, Bull Information Systems and lectured throughout the United States, as well as in Germany, France, Hong Kong, and Australia.

After moving to Virginia Beach, Virginia, she served as an adjunct professor in Public Speaking for Tidewater Community College and directed the speakers program for Edgar Cayce's Association for Research and Enlightenment (A.R.E.), where Una also conducted speaker training classes for eleven years. She's written four kindle books on the art of public speaking the first of which is entitled, *Create Your Speech*, available on Amazon. After 20 years of meticulous research, Una has seamlessly integrated an enormous body of information on Lemuria and brought to fruition a most important compilation of knowledge and insight in a highly readable, inspiring, and extraordinary book about a pre-recorded civilization that disappeared from the planet over 52,000 years ago.

Printed in the United States
By Bookmasters